DON'T TRY THIS AT HOME

DON'T TRY THIS AT HOME

HAROLD F. HAASER

TATE PUBLISHING
AND ENTERPRISES, LLC

Don't Try This at Home
Copyright © 2015 by Harold F. Haaser. All rights reserved.

No part of this publication may be reproduced, stored in a retrieval system or transmitted in any way by any means, electronic, mechanical, photocopy, recording or otherwise without the prior permission of the author except as provided by USA copyright law.

This book is designed to provide accurate and authoritative information with regard to the subject matter covered. This information is given with the understanding that neither the author nor Tate Publishing, LLC is engaged in rendering legal, professional advice. Since the details of your situation are fact dependent, you should additionally seek the services of a competent professional.

The opinions expressed by the author are not necessarily those of Tate Publishing, LLC.

Published by Tate Publishing & Enterprises, LLC
127 E. Trade Center Terrace | Mustang, Oklahoma 73064 USA
1.888.361.9473 | www.tatepublishing.com

Tate Publishing is committed to excellence in the publishing industry. The company reflects the philosophy established by the founders, based on Psalm 68:11,
"The Lord gave the word and great was the company of those who published it."

Book design copyright © 2015 by Tate Publishing, LLC. All rights reserved.
Cover design by Levimar & Company and Ivan Charlem Igot
Interior design by Jomar Ouano

Published in the United States of America

ISBN: 978-1-68028-797-4
Biography & Autobiography / Personal Memoirs
15.02.03

Acknowledgments

I would like to dedicate this book to my dad who loved me but never received a chance to enjoy this book.

To my brother who has laughed with me throughout my life.

To my wife and best friend, Sheryl, for believing in me and inspiring me and being a godly, gorgeous, and supporting wife.

To the Lord Almighty for granting me the wisdom, grace, and knowledge to make this happen.

Special thanks to Levimar & Company in Lakeland, Florida, for all the help on the fabulous cover.

Thanks to the Tate Publishing crew for all their knowledge and hard work during this delicate time.

Contents

1	Target Practice	11
2	Bike Accident	15
3	Will That Burn?	19
4	The Promotional Ruler	23
5	Fire!	27
6	What Blueprints?	31
7	The Last House on the Right	35
8	Adult Tree House	39
9	My First Motorcycle	43
10	Wet Shoes and More	47
11	Flammable	51
12	Four Wheels and Two Legs	53
13	Explosives and Stuff!	57
14	Croquet, Anyone?	65

15	Candy Hoist!	69
16	Grandma's Lead Foot	73
17	Christmas Lights	77
18	Kidnapping	83
19	Bat Attack	87
20	Best Easter Ever	93
21	Street Magic	97
22	Christmas Time	101
23	Escaping Nap Time	105
24	New Bedrooms	109
25	Boy Scout Memories	113
26	Early Age Technology	119
27	Weeds and Gas and Fire, Oh My!	125
28	Life in the Basement	129
29	007	133
30	I Never Inhaled	137
31	It Wasn't Me!	139
32	Fireworks to Rockets	141
33	Big Red Tomatoes	147
34	Dangerous Maintenance	151
35	The Chello	155
36	Trash Eliminators	159
37	Big Band Sounds	163
38	Beer Trucks	167
39	Quiet on the Set	171
40	Dumpsters Aren't All Bad	177

41	Accidental Runover	181
42	Angels from Heaven	185
43	School Fight	189
44	Chemistry Class	193
45	Unlimited Embarrassment	195
46	Deer Tracks	197
47	Uncle Bob	203
48	The Johnny Carson Show	207

Synopsis 215
About the Author 217

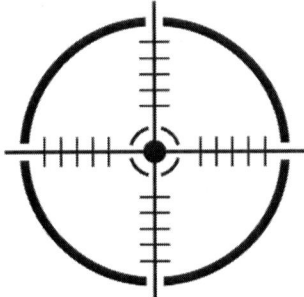

1

Target Practice

You have probably at one time or another watched the movie *Home Alone*. I have similar stories to share about being "home alone." My parents were avid bingo players. It didn't matter what town, what day, what time, or how far away bingo gatherings were, my parents drove there and played the game. I would venture to say they drove a one hundred and fifty mile radius from our house. This was a six-day-a-week project. Every "bingo" day, time and location was mapped out on our kitchen calendar, hanging next to the hooks for the car keys.

One Saturday, I was home alone and bored, so I started snooping around the house. First I went through both of my sister's bedrooms and then my mom and dad's. Nothing was found new or interesting, so I moved on to my brother's bedroom.

While searching his bedroom, I looked in his dresser and under the bed but didn't find much. Then I hit the jackpot! I opened up his closet doors and saw a rifle bag way in the back, carefully covered with some of his clothes, leaning up in the corner. I didn't know he had a rifle! Could this be a BB gun or maybe even better, a pellet gun? I opened the crisp, clean leather-looking rifle bag and saw an instrument of power. I knew the rifle had to be powerful because it had a scope mounted right on the barrel. He even had cute little bullets I found that fit right in the chamber. I thought to myself, *These bullets couldn't be too powerful because they're so small.* I didn't know at the time it was a .22 rifle used for target practice. I put one of the bullets in a vice in the garage and pulled the head off with my dad's pair of pliers. Once I got the head of the bullet off, I wondered what was at the bottom and stuck a small screwdriver in and scratched around, and the gun powder ignited and scorched my eyebrows. I learned never to do that again! I was so excited to see what the rifle could do. I loaded a new bullet in the barrel and ran into my bedroom. I had some difficulty removing the screen from my window, but after some heavy tugging, I finally bent the corner and got it off. Now I was cooking. I'm the man! I've got the power! I laid the rifle on the window ledge and looked down through the scope. Wow, I thought, *This is so cool!*

I could see our pool shed and beyond, and everything looked so close. I thought the little bullet would at least hit the pool shed from this distance. I looked through the scope, and through the crosshair, I could see the white aluminum siding on the shed and took aim and squeezed the trigger. I was surprised there was very little noise and not much of a kick, but it seemed like a zillionth of a second after I pulled the trigger and smoke came rolling out of the barrel, I saw something pass by in the scope. I lowered the rifle just a bit, and to my surprise, I saw my brother walk around the corner! If I had waited one second more, I would have killed him. I was scared to death, not because I almost killed my brother, but because he almost caught me with his rifle! I hurried and closed up my window and ran back to my brother's bedroom and threw the rifle back in the case, slammed the closet doors, and ran outside. I thought I better get out of the house and go investigate the pool shed.

As I ran out of the house, my brother was walking up the sidewalk and asked why I was in a hurry. I told him I was going to get something out of the shed. As I approached the age-old shed, I could see a small black dent with a hole in the white aluminum siding. I pulled open the shed door and saw the projectile "right of way" starting with a hole through the backing of the aluminum siding, through the pool umbrella, and through a plastic bucket hanging from a ceiling hook. I immediately began to pull everything out of the shed so no one would be able to match up the damage. About halfway through pulling the bullet-riddled items out of the shed, my parents arrived back from the proverbial bingo game. Both my mom and dad could see me as they pulled into the garage. Both of them commented at the same time, "Look at our youngest son cleaning out the pool shed, and we didn't even have to ask him!" They were very pleased, proud, and excited that I took the initiative to do such a task at my age.

It seemed like only seconds after they entered the house, I heard a deep bellow from my dad calling my name, which could be heard throughout the neighborhood. I ran up to the house acting like I didn't know why they would be calling me. After all, I was cleaning out the pool shed! When I arrived in the kitchen, my mother, father, and brother were waiting. My brother was holding his rifle. No one had a smile on their face. Then the question came ringing out, "Did you shoot your brother's rifle?" This was the exact moment in my life when I figured out that if you cry and look sad, you can get away with almost anything. I started crying and mumbled, "Mom and Dad, I've been out cleaning the pool shed. I didn't shoot any dumb rifle!" I could see in their eyes they believed every word that came out of my mouth, and for that one moment, I was finally the good son!

My brother roared up and said, "But, Mom, I ejected the shell, and smoke came out of the rifle."

My mom quickly interrupted and said, "You probably left the bullet in there from the last time you shot it."

Thank goodness my mom didn't know anything about guns. The discussion was over, and my brother went back to his bedroom irritated. My mom began to prepare supper, and I went back to cleaning the shed. The best thing that happened was, I never got a whooping! The rest of that evening went well, and as I finished cleaning the shed, I was thinking how I faked the cry and got away with not getting a spanking. I never realized that day that I could have easily killed my brother!

2

Bike Accident

My bike was a hand-me-down, complete with wrinkled fenders, scuffed up red paint, thick worn tires, and cardboard in the spokes secured with beat up wood clothes pins. One day, I was ridding up and down our dead end street wearing a pair of red waxed lips I received from a school birthday. When you're a kid and you get a set of wax lips, you try to wear them as long as you can, biting the inside wax and flashing them to everyone you pass by. I bit into the lips a hundred times, and now it was time to just go ahead and chew them up. Once you get the lips loaded into your mouth, it's hard to talk, let alone breathe through your mouth. After the red lips were chewed up, I gave them a spit with all my might, and the huge red wad landed on my neighbor's fresh cut lawn. He would never know what the red mass was or how it got there, so I continued to ride my bike trying to see how fast I could go. I noticed my brother was approaching me on his bike, and he quickly turned around and rode with me for a minute and then said, "Hey, bet you can't catch me!"

Nobody could beat my red rocket, so I said okay and gave it everything I had, and in no time, I was almost caught up. I was proud of my red rocket because it was my first adult bike, and it sounded like a motorcycle. My brother peddled into our driveway and veered right, and I was right behind him. Inch by inch, I was gaining on him as I felt the wind blow past my face at this incredible speed. I followed him around our backyard, almost passing him as our speeds escalated to supersonic. My brother aimed his bike for the side door of the garage, but I didn't realize what he was up to. As he approached the door, he slowed down, allowing me to get just a bit closer. He maneuvered through the side of the garage, grabbed the sun-baked entrance door with his right hand, and slammed it as hard as he could, seconds before I arrived. Everything seemed to be in slow motion, just like in the old western movies when the bad guys would blow up a bridge just as the train reached the halfway mark, and everything would fall in slow motion and smash into a million pieces. For me, there was no time to slam on the brakes, no time to initiate a shutdown on my red rocket control panel, no time to pull the lever for the safety parachutes. I had to face the cold reality that I was about to hit that door at an enormous speed, and there was nothing I could do about it. As the front of the red rocket struck the door, I had one eye closed, and my other eye just had to see what was going to happen. As if I was in space floating with no gravity, I saw in slow motion the door brake away from the rusty colored hinges and slam into the concrete floor and brake into a million pieces, just like the train wreck. As I hit the concrete, suddenly everything became quiet as dust and microscopic wood fragments settled on my face. I felt a little pain as I lay silently on the dirty cold concrete, gathering my thoughts. The scariest thought that entered my head was, *What was my mom and dad going to say when they saw the door that once stood tall, keeping all the elements out and providing service for our family all these years?* As I got up, I was suddenly more concerned about the red rocket rather than the small cut and blood on my head. I heard laughter from afar, and as I looked up, I saw my brother at the other end of the four-car garage sitting on his bike with his arms crossed.

"You're in big trouble," he said with a smirk on his face. "Who do you think Mom and Dad are going to believe…you or me?"

He was right! I was in so much trouble growing up; there's no way they'll believe me. He told me to clean up the mess I made, and he was going in to watch TV. As I picked up the pieces and swept the floor, I started to get scared and wondered if I would ever see daylight again. I'd be grounded for life! After cleaning up, I examined the red rocket and saw the front wheel was almost bent in half. I dragged it to the corner of the garage and decided to go in the house and get my punishment over with. Surprisingly, the atmosphere in the house was calm, and my mom and dad along with my brother were watching TV. I went directly to my bedroom and waited for my punishment, not knowing when my brother would break the news to my parents. I waited in my room, which seemed like a year, before I heard my brother coming down the hall. He walked in the room with a big smile on his face and told me the story about the wind blowing the door shut, which conveniently worked, and I was off the hook. He said my dad told him the door was old anyway, and he was thinking about getting it replaced. My brother was laughing as he left the room and said I owed him big time. I never thought my brother had it in him to stick up for me and come up with a great story. I did however have to work most of the summer to save up enough money to replace the front wheel of the red rocket. I guess my brother was all right after all…or was he?

3

Will That Burn?

One rainy day during our summer break from grade school, one of my jobs was to sweep out the garage, which at the time was empty because my dad was at work, and my mom left her car parked in the driveway. The detached four-car garage cement floor was filthy. We didn't have a lawn blower to blow out the debris, so I had to sweep it out with an old corn broom. While I was inhaling the dust fumes bouncing off the concrete floor, I had a great idea. I watched countless TV programs where someone had accidentally started a fire and threw a blanket on top to smother the flames. I could try that experiment very easily! We had barbecue matches for starting the grill; we had gasoline from the lawn mower. Why not pour gas on the floor and see what it does? I was totally cool with this experiment because the garage floor was concrete, and I knew it couldn't burn! I got the gasoline and poured out a large amount on the center of the floor and set it ablaze! It was cool! The roaring flames danced higher and higher, almost reaching the drywall ceiling! There was black smoke floating aimlessly in the air, and the concrete floor actually looked like it was burning.

Then I remembered I forgot one thing.

I needed something to throw over the roaring fire. The only item lying around in the garage was our custom-made waterproof car tarp we used to cover luggage on top of our Mercury station wagon. We always used the tarp when we went on family vacations, and I thought the tarp would work even better than a blanket because it was thicker. I hurried and threw the canvas tarp on top of the roaring fire, but it didn't put it out like in the movies. To my surprise, the tarp started on fire. Now I got scared! The flames were producing a lot of thick smoke, and the air inside of the garage was getting hard to breathe. I had a four-alarm fire in our garage, and no one around to help. My plan wasn't working, and I was going to have a big problem real soon! Somehow I dragged the burning canvas car top out on the driveway and ran to get the water hose. Once I got the hose on full blast and put out the fiery inferno, I realized that the canvas tarp would never be the same. The evidence was riddled with black holes, which burned through almost fifty percent of the tarp. It looked like a black piece of Swiss cheese. I had to think fast because at any time, my mom could glance out the window and see the truth! I quickly grabbed a shovel and dragged the Swiss cheese tarp behind the garage. We had a huge field behind the garage where we played army and other fun games, but today, I was going to use it as a hiding place. There were lots of dirt and weeds and small trees, which gave me the coverage I needed so my mom couldn't see me. I started to dig a hole faster than a backhoe. I finally dug down to a million feet, threw the burned evidence in the deep dark hole, and started to fill it back up. I didn't want to leave any evidence, so I hurried and was surprised how fast I covered the hole. I cleaned the shovel off and put it back in the garage, finished sweeping out the ashes and dirt, and made the garage look better than it ever had.

    The next day, I received a "good job" when my mom inspected it, never asking why I left all the garage doors open that night. We never took another vacation where we needed the car tarp again, and I think it's still buried in that field to this day.

4

The Promotional Ruler

As far back as I can remember, I've always been told I was a little mischievous and was titled the black sheep of the family. Being young, I didn't really know what that meant nor did I care; I was just having fun. I remember one time when my brother and I were in our bedroom, and we couldn't sleep. We were telling jokes and clowning around, and then I came up with a great idea to pass the time. I explained my plans to make a human bridge across the two beds! I convinced my brother to stretch across the beds since he was older and stronger, and I would be the one to walk across being younger and weighing less. Do you have this visual? We thought we were pretty cool as my brother stretched across the beds now becoming the human bridge. I started to walk across his body, balancing myself now in the middle of his back, when suddenly, the bedroom door flew open and slammed against the wall. With the room still dark, my dad started to lay into us about the noise and how late it was. He stood at the door quietly for a moment and then flipped on the light switch and saw the human bridge under construction.

My brother's back started to give way and later commented that he was ready to puke from my weight on his back. My brother gave it all he had and hear I was, still standing on his back and acting like I'm sleeping standing up. "This was Harold's idea, Dad," my brother grunted.

Needless to say, I really got in trouble. I remember one time, my mom received a free "promotional ruler" from the bank; and while spanking me one day, it suddenly broke. I stopped crying and was proud my behind was tougher than her ruler. Seconds later, my dream faded as she pulled out a second promotional ruler from the kitchen drawer. Evidently, you could get more than one from the bank! I also remember when we bought a brand-new orange tree and planted it in the backyard. When I found out it was an orange tree, I got pretty excited thinking we could go pick our own oranges and make orange juice. When I arrived in the backyard, the tree was very small and had no oranges. I thought for a minute and figured maybe I could help the little tree grow faster and went into the house and brought out five or six oranges we had in a bowl in the kitchen. I taped the oranges at the end of the limbs with fifty pounds of scotch tape, thinking I was showing the tree what to grow.

The next morning, my mom asked what happened to all the oranges in the bowel; and me being proud of my idea of helping the little tree, spoke up and explained what I did. My mom went out to get the oranges and came back really mad. Evidently, the oranges were too heavy and broke all the little tree limbs; and so my good deed went unnoticed, and once again I saw the promotional ruler. I was so upset that I walked out the front door and yelled I'm running away from home and slammed the door as hard as I could.

As I walked past house after house, it seemed like hours had gone by, and it also felt like someone was watching me; but I looked in the windows of each house I passed, and no one was there. I didn't know then that my dad was following me and hiding behind trees as I neared the first intersection. At the intersection was a grocery store with a candy display in the front window. I figured I would go in and look, even though I didn't have any money. As I struggled to open the large wooden door, I finally arrived inside where I could smell something sweet, and my eyes were drawn to all the candy in the antique glass case. There was a million pieces of every candy you could think of and then some that I had never seen before. As I stared at the candy and saliva ran out of the corners of my mouth, the lady behind the counter asked if she could help me. I said no thanks and never looked up, but all the time, my dad was outside pointing at me and keeping in contact with the lady behind the counter. After I gazed at every row of candy a couple of times, the kind lady asked me if I was ready to go back home. The lady looked a little like my grandmother and was very nice to me, and so when I forgot why I ran away from home and said I was leaving, she gave me a piece of penny candy, and I tore off the wrapper as fast as I could. I never forgot the butterscotch flavor that filled my senses, and I felt like a new person! As I struggled with the large wooden door once again to get outside, I started home skipping and enjoying my free piece of candy and couldn't quite remember the whole story of why I was running away.

Later in life, my new wife and I went to Las Vegas so she could meet my dad for the first time. After meeting him, my wife excused herself to use the restroom, and I felt his hand slam across my chest. As I looked over to my dad, he was smiling from his wheel chair and said, "Where did you find her? She's beautiful!" That was the last time my dad ever hit me, but this time I didn't mind it.

5

Fire!

My dad and his brothers owned a beer distributing company. As a young boy, sometimes I was allowed to ride with a driver to a beer distributing company in another state. I was so amazed at the size of the buildings and all the trucks and forklifts and all the different bottle sizes and colors. I think when you're young, everything looks bigger. On Saturdays, my brother and I would wash the beer trucks for twenty-five cents an hour, and we thought we were cool. Those trucks seemed twenty feet tall, and I did all I could to reach the top with a soapy brush to clean off the dirt. Using the hose to rinse off the soap was the easy part. I remember seeing a Black Label bottle that was shaped like a keg, and the bottle stuck in my head because it looked so cool. If I drank beer, I would have chosen that bottle to drink it out of! The bottle fit in my hand perfectly, and I knew I could use it for something!

About three weeks later, I was home watching an army show on TV, and I noticed an army guy throw a bottle, with a rag stuffed in it on fire, into a house, and it started the house on fire. Wow! I thought that was so cool, and the bottle reminded me of the keg bottle I saw at the warehouse! I was excited! I began to dream about what I could do with five or six of those bottles.

The next time my brother and I went to the warehouse to wash trucks, I smuggled three of the "keg" bottles home safely and warehoused them in my bedroom. Now for my mission! I waited until bingo night and knew my parents were gone. Next, I went into the bathroom, stuffed a washcloth in my pocket, emptied the stinky beer into the sink, and rinsed the bottles thoroughly. I took one bottle with me in the garage and filled it with gasoline from the lawn mower and stuffed the washcloth inside the bottle, just like the army guys. I took a handful of matches from the barbecue grill and hiked down to the river. The turnpike bridge was huge and very tall and was held up over the river by huge concrete pillars. I made my way down the hill, crossed over the rusty railroad tracks, and got as close to the water as I could before I could set up the launch! I remember it was a still, quiet night, and I could hear the cars roaring overhead on the Turnpike as the night slowly got darker. I was nervous and wondered if I could make the long throw. I reached in my pocket for the matches only to see some had broken in half. *That's okay*, I thought, *they'll still light*. I reached for a big stone to strike the first one. No luck. It blew out. The second match blew out as well. Finally, on the third try, I started the gasoline soaked fuse, and the flame started to roar and snap in the cool dark evening air. I'll never forget that feeling of power. I threw the blazing bottle with all my might, and it sailed threw the air, over the water, and finally smashed with precise accuracy, and gas ran down the pillar seconds before it caught on fire. The flames lit up the sky. The cars driving under the bridge began to slow down as they viewed the dancing flames, thinking the bridge was on fire. I was hidden by the tall weeds and was never detected by the slow-paced vehicles.

The energized flames lasted about three or four minutes, but as a young boy, it seemed like a half hour! As the blazes subsided, leaving its blackened trail on the white concrete pillar, the night returned to dark once again, and everything went back to normal. The experiment went down without a hitch, and I hiked back home thinking of what I would create next!

6

What Blueprints?

As a young boy, I always liked to play in the field behind our house. We were fortunate to have a forest like area full of trees and weeds, a perfect place to play army or just hike through. The forest, which later was turned into a mobile home park, was very long and wide and went from our backyard, clear out to the turnpike. It was great! I couldn't wait until summer when school was out so I could build a fort and sleep in it. Those were the days. One year, my dad surprised me for my birthday and brought home a dump truck load of scraps from the lumberyard.

My dad knew the owner at the lumber yard, and he gave my dad scarps for free when he told him it was for my birthday. I was in heaven! I saw four by eight sheets of plywood, two by fours—you name it, and it was there. I hauled every stick of that lumber by hand out to my new "construction site." I had the lumber, a hammer, some nails, and a handsaw and was ready to start construction. I took four by fours and buried them in the ground, which was my foundation for the rest of the fort. I began to nail a sheet of plywood on top of the four by fours for the floor. Later I nailed plywood on the sides, and finally, I was ready for the last sheet, which made the roof. The fort construction took me about ten days to complete. I built a ladder to reach the trap door for access into the fort. I also dug a hole right next to the ladder under the fort and called it a basement. We had an old metal chair at home, which I smuggled out and nailed to a piece of plywood and laid it on top of the hole. After that, I covered the plywood with dirt to keep it my secret room. If you wanted access to the basement, tip the chair, and the plywood would open, and I would jump in. I had handles on the inside to pull the door shut and had birthday candles for electricity. It was great!

The next day, I asked my mom if she would take me to the local carpet store to pick up discontinued carpet samples. To make a long story short, the sales guy knew my mom and gave me a big box of discontinued samples. I was in heaven once again! I couldn't get home fast enough to start installing the carpet. I nailed carpet to the ceiling, the walls, and the floor. This was my first soundproof fort.

Later that week, my dad asked me if I had made blueprints for the fort. Right away I said no and then asked what blueprints are, because I didn't remember seeing anything blue while I was at the construction site. He then explained when carpenters build a home, they need these blueprints to figure out how to build the structure. I started thinking about what my dad said and figured I needed some blueprints too, so after lunch, I got some paper and started drawing my blueprints. I had one heck of a time scotch taping piece after piece to each other to make it as large as the fort. I was using a "number four" crayon, brown to match some of the wood, and finally by the end of the day finished my blueprint. I rolled it up and put a rubber band on it, just like the big guys! I showed my dad, and I thought he looked impressed; but little did I know, he didn't want to hurt my feelings. The next morning came quickly. After eating breakfast, I ran out to the construction site to finish the carpet installation. It took a lot of nails, but I finished, and it looked good as long as you didn't stare at the nails that came through the wood on the outside of the fort. Very colorful!

Now came the big moment in my life—to live, sleep, and play in the fort. I built this fort for four people! All summer long, my friends and I played in this ninth wonder of the world. We had all kinds of wars and games, and the fort protected us all! I even got in the basement and lit candles, and no one knew I was down there. Then winter set in. It was time to bring in the sleeping bags and shut the fort down until next year. It was a sad time. As winter progressed, we had a couple of big storms with lots and lots of snow and tremendous winds. We had several days off because the schools were closed down. One Saturday, I got up and looked out the window only to see piles and piles of snow. As I ran out of the house to start to play, I looked out at the fort, but it wasn't there! Instantly, I thought one of the neighbor kids stole my fort. As I hiked over the deep drifts, I arrived at the construction site only to see a few scraps of wood remaining. I couldn't believe it! All that hard work and now it's gone, just like that!

As the snow melted that year, I never did find all the lumber. I looked in the basement, and all the candles were floating in water. The carpet samples were gone as well as the lawn chair attached to the secret trap door. I never built another fort after that winter, but I still saved the blueprints.

7

The Last House on the Right

My family lived in the country and on a dead-end street. I guess the correct verbiage today is a "no outlet" street. When turning into our no outlet street, the grass was tall enough to hide someone. My cousin and I would hide in the tall weeds during Halloween, and when the kids from other neighborhoods were leaving our street, we would jump up in our costume, scaring them and telling them to give us a hand full of candy or they couldn't leave.

At the other end of our dead-end street was an older scary-looking two-story home, like the Adams family's house on TV. It could have been a farm house at one time with a huge porch and an old squeaky stairs that lead to the front door. I always remembered those squeaky stairs from the good old trick or treat days. One thing that would make the hair on the back of my neck stand up was a porcelain frog on the front porch that gave me the willies. I remembered watching a scary movie one time, and it had a big monster frog, like the one on the porch, and it scared me to death! The giant frog ended up eating all the people in town and the army trucked in all kinds of machine guns and tanks to kill it. The frog statue had eyes that looked like they were following you wherever you walked on the porch. I even came up behind it one time, and when I came around to the front, there it was staring at me. I used to have nightmares about me being on the porch, and all of a sudden, the frog came to life and was chasing me down the street.

One day I was climbing in a tree in our front yard and reached as far up as I could climb because the limbs were getting thinner, and I could hear some cracking noise. I stopped and nestled in between the thicker limbs and noticed I was higher then I had ever climbed a tree before. As the silent wind blew past my face, the tree swayed back and forth. It was a gentle sway, and I felt all cozy and safe. Seated at the top of the tree I could see forever, and as I surveyed my neighborhood all the way around the tree, I noticed way down at the end of the street I could see the Adams family's house, and everyone was loading into their car. It was so cool to see them, but no one detected me nestled high above the clouds in our front yard. I watched as the entire family loaded up in their station wagon and drove right past me and left our street. I started thinking, *How could that family live there all this time and not be afraid of the frog!* Maybe they never saw the show! Maybe they never had bad dreams about it! Maybe it never chased them down the street! I had a great idea now that the coast was clear, and I slowly made my way down the huge tree, making sure my footing was exact on each limb. I launched myself off the tree once I reached the bottom and surveyed the neighborhood to make sure no one was watching me. I ran with all my might to the end of the street, not knowing how much time I had left before the Adams family would arrive back home. Maybe they went to get groceries or went for a drive, or maybe they were getting another frog!

Trying to catch my breath as I walked up the squeaky steps, out of the corner of my eye, I saw the monster frog still looking at my every move. I decided to act like I didn't see it and walked the long way around the porch. Once past the frog and safe, I toughened up and started running toward the back of the frog so he couldn't see me; and once within reach, I grabbed the porcelain statue, raised it as high as I could above my head, and with all my might slammed it to the porch floor, watching it break into a million pieces. Big pieces and little pieces were scattered all over the porch. Some traveled into flower pots, and others made it off the porch and into the deep grass.

There was no way that anyone from the Adams family could ever put this nightmare together again. And to make sure, I took a few pieces with me and put them in our garbage can! Now the neighborhood was safe again, and it was nice to know the Adams family never replaced the statue.

8

Adult Tree House

My brother and I were playing touch football in our front yard one summer day, and we were losing big time. We were playing with two older brothers who lived at the end of the street in a scary house I named the Adams family's house. I don't remember why we were playing football with them; I just remember them being bigger and stronger than we were.

After getting beat up and losing the game, everyone started to go home when one of the Adams family brothers asked if I wanted to see their tree house. I loved forts, so I jumped right in and said yes. I raced him over to their backyard, and of course, him being older, he beat me by a landslide. When I arrived in his backyard, I was amazed how scary it was and how high the grass had grown. It was so high you almost couldn't see the broken down bicycles and lawn mowers nestled in the grass. The air smelled like they had a dog, and the entire backyard was his bathroom. I kept looking down at my shoes to see if I had any surprises clinging on for dear life. As I made my way over to the tree watching every step I took, I happened to look up, and there it was! This mammoth tree housed a two-room small home. It was huge, and I have no idea how they built it or how long it took them. The only way up or down was by a rope that was very thick, had no knots to hang on to, and looked like it was a million feet long. The older boy climbed the giant rope in seconds, and as he looked down, must have felt sorry for me and told me to hang on, and he'd pull me up. I grabbed the rope like it was no big deal but was scared to death and hanging on for my life. The time I spent traveling up the rope was very fast, almost as if I was launched into the air by rocket power. I made it to the top of this monster tree without letting go of the rope and was amazed how far up I was and how big the tree was. This palace had two rooms with carpet and everything! The fort was the best fort in the whole world! As I was looking around in the first room, I noticed a hole in the wall facing the turnpike. As I peered through it, I could see the field and the cars on the turnpike and thought, *What a great view from way up here.* I asked if they use this spy hole to check if any one's attacking the tree house.

The older boy responded, "No, that's where we go pee."

Instantly, I pulled my face away and acted like I knew that and then changed the subject. As I moved into the second room, I was in shock to see picture after picture of girls with no clothes on, plastered on the walls. It was like wallpaper on each wall of the room. That was the first time I ever saw such a thing! It seemed like hours looking at those pictures when my concentration was broken.

The older boy said, "Come on. I'll lower you back down."

I didn't really want to go after what I just saw and was still in amazement as he lowered me to the ground. As I walked home still stunned, I thought to myself, *How did he get those clothes off those girls?* I had never seen anything like that before in my life. He must have used a pencil eraser. Yes, I thought that's what he did. I solved my own mystery! So I raced home and grabbed the JC Penny catalog and headed for my bedroom. I started to use my school pencil eraser on the bra section of the magazine. I erased and erased until there were holes in the pages. I couldn't get the clothes off! I couldn't understand what was wrong. Then it came to me. I'm erasing the wrong type of book! That's what it is! I ran out of my bedroom and got a *Sears* magazine and started to work on those girls but with the same results, holes in the pages. I was very frustrated and thought maybe the older boy had some special eraser.

That was the last time I was ever in the tree house, and I never found out the real answer about the eraser until I grew up years later.

9

My First Motorcycle

As I grew older and had my tenth birthday, I began to notice girls. They were very different than boys! They were cute. They smelled good, never got dirty, and I didn't mind talking to them. Of course, when you live on a dead-end street, you don't have much to choose from.

One day, I didn't have anything to do, so I had an idea to mount an old lawn mower engine we had in the pool shed on the front of my bike. I saw something that looked like it, in a *Popular Science* magazine one time when I was getting a haircut. I walked back to our faded sun beaten shed and started digging through all the junk that accumulated throughout the years. Finally after about twenty minutes, I hit the jackpot and found the old engine and traveled back to the garage, changing hands every ten feet because it was so heavy. I called my brother outside and asked him to give me a hand. He was older and had all the tools and the know-how on just about anything mechanical. After explaining what I saw in the magazine, he smiled and said he could build this contraption. I told him I preferred to call it my motorcycle! He dug through some scrap he had in the garage from working on his car, and after some grinding, drilling, and using the vise on his work table, he made the brackets to hold the engine on the front of the bike. We spent the rest of the day figuring out how the motor would connect to the bike and how to install the throttle and a million other things.

I awoke the next day only to find out I was the last one to get up! My brother had eaten breakfast and was already working on the motorcycle. My mom made me eat breakfast before I could go outside, so I inhaled my cereal as fast as I could, and I know some of the frosted flakes never touched my throat. I skidded the empty bowel across the countertop and ran as fast as I could to the garage. As my legs came to a screeching halt, to my surprise, my brother had completed the installation. Everything on the bike was completed, and he was tightening up the last bolt.

The next step was to fire up the engine, and my brother had a smile on his face as he pointed to the ragged pull rope. This was the minute I was waiting for, and on the second pull, the old lawn mower engine came to life. It sounded loud and blew a lot of smoke, but I was ready for my maiden voyage. I climbed aboard and slowly pushed the handmade throttle forward. I began to move slowly and had a grin from ear to ear. I traveled off our driveway and out onto the street where I gave it full throttle and my motorcycle took off. I thought I was traveling near a hundred miles an hour, but my brother said it was more like ten miles per hour. I knew I had the sweetest thing on wheels! It was getting time for supper, so I drove my motorized invention into the garage and parked it by my brother's car.

The next morning arrived quickly, and I woke up excited. After breakfast, I decided to shine up my motor cycle because I had a big day ahead of me and a lot of people to show off for. I look back now and think how in the world did I ever shine that bike up? First of all, it was a hand-me-down with hardly any red paint left on the frame, two wheels that didn't match, a twenty-five-pound motor hanging over to one side, and bent handlebars. I guess when you're young, you don't really pay attention to those things. I fired up my new transportation and headed for the street. I must have driven up and down the street for hours. The engine was loud, the steering was pulling to one side, and I smelled like a gasoline exhaust. As I traveled to the stop sign to turn around, I noticed one of those girls who always smelled good I was talking about earlier, and she was standing at the end of her driveway staring at me. She was about three years younger and had long black hair and was always dressed nicely. As I started back down the street for the millionth time, I acted like I didn't see her and cruised by at top speed. I was up and down that street so many times I had every stone and grass blade memorized, but she didn't know that, so I acted cool by not waving. As I turned around this time, I decided to head her way to see if she thought I was cool on my motorcycle. As I slowed down at the entrance to her driveway, I noticed she was looking the other way. I pulled up and revved the engine a few times to let her know who's in town, and then shut down my rig. She turned around and I said hi and she just looked at me. I asked if she liked my motorcycle and also told her I noticed she was staring at me when I drove by.

She laughed and said, "Not really. I was looking for the mailman because my mother sent me out to wait for him." She also explained in the same breath that I smelled terrible.

I was so embarrassed I got back on my motorcycle and peddled it all the way home forgetting to start the motor. I put the motorcycle back in the garage and didn't drive it for about a week. Luckily, about three months later, her whole family moved, and I didn't have to be embarrassed any more!

10

Wet Shoes and More

If you live in the real world and have brothers or sisters, you know that things don't always go well. There are good times, and there are bad times. An example of a good time in our house was when I got home from school early and spotted a cake inside a plastic cake dispenser. I would carefully open the lid and cut a small hole and remove the first layer of cake with the frosting on it and then hollow out the inside. After I ate my fill, I slid the first piece I saved back into the cake and frosted it back together so no one could see the difference.

    An example of a bad time would be when I asked my brother how he moved his nostrils without touching them and he said, "If I tell you, what will you give me?" I told him I would give him my favorite bag of marbles because I really wanted to learn this trick. He said okay, and I gave him the marbles, and as he stood up and put them in his pocket, he said, "Move a muscle in your nose," and walked out the door. I started crying, but no one would be one my side.

One day, my brother and I got into a fight and he pushed me and I accidently hit the dresser and hurt my elbow. I wanted to get back, so I waited until he left the house the next day and went into his bedroom and peed in one of his shoes! The shoes were his favorite because they had the leather heals, and when you walked on a hard surface, you could hear a click noise on the sidewalk or on concrete, and back then that was cool!

The next day came around, and believe it or not, the fluid either soaked in or evaporated because it was bone-dry, and he wore them to school. I never said anything about the shoes until we were adults and made sure it was on a phone call. I still don't know if he really believed that story, but he did bring up another story about the time he was building an aircraft-carrier model. The model itself was at least three feet long, and I know he was really proud of it. The carrier had flight pilots standing up, lift elevators with planes parked on them, and the lifts actually went up and down the craft by turning a knob on the side of the ship. There were machine guns, radio equipment, helicopters, troops of soldiers, you name it and it was on the ship.

Several months after the craft was completed, we had gotten into an argument, and naturally, he won. I wanted to get back at him, so later that day, I snuck back into the basement when he was gone and broke the wings off a few of the planes. About a month later, I had forgotten all about the fight, and my brother went back into the basement to get something and found the disaster. He ran upstairs and told my mom, and she called me on the carpet. I had to admit to her I must have accidently bumped into it, and she told me I had to replace it with my own money.

The next day, my mom was running some errands and drove me to our hometown hobby shop. Luckily, my mom didn't really pay attention to what size my brother's model was, so when I picked one out for five dollars and ninety nine cents, she thought that was just fine. We traveled back home, and I gave the model to my brother, and he flipped out complaining about the size and cost. My mom told him to quit arguing and be happy your brother replaced the model.

11

Flammable

I started assembling plastic model kits from our hometown Hobby Store at a young age after watching my brother build battle ships and hot rods. I remember like it was yesterday, the time I was gluing pieces of a model rocket together and tossed the glue tube back on the work bench and the word *flammable* stuck out like a neon light. I don't know why I never saw those words before; I guess because I never read the directions. I did know the glue had quite an order, and it glued my model together really fast.

I began to wonder if flammable meant it would burn inside the house. I was curious to find out, so while my model part was drying, I squirted a small test pattern on the concrete block walls in the basement and lit it with our barbecue matches. It started on fire immediately and spitted and spurted like a fuse on a firecracker. *Cool*, I thought. I wanted to expand my experiment to see just what this marvelous gel could do. I began to squeeze out long lines of this stinky flammable material up and down the basement block wall. I made a pretty cool design with a starting and ending point. I thought this time I'll turn off the lights to see the real effect of my invention. I may be on to something that maybe nobody else knows about, and I'll be some kind of a hero for developing this technique! I turned off the lights and lit the starting point of the glue pattern. It ignited instantly, and may I say proudly, it was spectacular! Very spectacular, in fact I thought I may have outdone myself! The trail of glue seemed to burn forever with sparkles and flames following the pattern I had designed. When the awesome show was over, I turned on the lights and almost had a heart attack! The trail of fun left a huge black mark all over the wall, and there were tiny black ashes floating all over the basement. I thought to myself that this "flammable" stuff should only burn outside, but it was too late now. I knew I had to do something fast because I was in big trouble. I immediately began to move the spare refrigerator, the workbench, and all sorts of furniture over to the crime scene to cover the blacken wall.

About the time I moved the last piece into position and was sweeping up those nasty ashes, the basement door opened and my Mom said, "What are you doing down there?"

I quickly responded I was cleaning the basement while my model parts were drying. She said okay and closed the basement door. That night at the supper table, she told my dad about me cleaning the basement, and he gave me a big smile and told me I was doing a great job helping out around the house. After supper, I was walking to my room thinking this time I received some brownie points, and no one found out. I'm pretty sure that was the last time any of the basement furniture was ever moved until the house was sold years later.

12

Four Wheels and Two Legs

My brother was the first child in our family, and he got everything he wanted and settled into the "good life." Three years later, I arrived. My brother, not having any other siblings and not knowing how to handle this new "brother thing," became jealous. Now he had to learn to share his toys and accept the fact my parents were sharing their love as well—it wasn't all about him any more. Let's just say he didn't adapt to the terminology very well, and I was the one who had to pay the price.

I was told a story about a cold winter day we were all at my grandmother's house. My brother couldn't go outside and play due to the snow and slippery ice, and he became bored. I was just learning how to walk at the time and was standing in one of those four-wheel walker carts. My brother strolled into the living room and grabbed a handful of cigarette butts from an ash tray my dad had been contributing to all day. With a hidden handful of half-smoked butts, my brother innocently traveled back into the kitchen where he found me surfing on the kitchen linoleum. He cornered me at the refrigerator and commenced packing cigarette butts in both of my ears. He said I was crying, but no one heard anything, and I always wondered why I was alone in the kitchen with him in the first place! After the cigarette butts were carefully loaded, he opened the basement door. My grandmother's basement steps weren't a straight set of carpeted steps; they were linoleum steps that went down about six or seven. Then there was a small landing to go outside and then the steps turned the corner and proceeded down another six or seven, and ended in the dark and scary basement that smelled like moth balls. My grandmother claimed keeping moth balls in the basement would keep mice and bats out. With the basement door wide open, my brother pushed me to the first step and let go of the walker and then proceeded to slam the door. *All gone,* he said to himself. At first I proceeded to slide down the steps in slow motion, but then the banging up against the wall started, and I was picking up momentum and turning some pretty good acrobatic flips. As I hit the landing bouncing off the back door, I proceeded to fly down to the last of the steps ending on the cold hard gray-colored concrete floor, home of the stinky moth balls. He said I was crying between the slamming of the door and banging of my walking cart against the wall traveling down the steps at a hundred miles an hour.

Luckily, my mom heard the commotion and ran into the kitchen. My brother was picking up the last of the cigarette evidence, and she screamed, "Where's your brother?"

Calmly throwing the last handful of tobacco in the trash can, he said I was in the basement. My mom ran down the basement steps, and sure enough she found me at the bottom crying and scared with a goose egg and a little blood on my nose. My brother didn't lie. He told the truth; I was in the basement. He told my mom he didn't want me around any more.

I don't remember any of that day, but I suppose he received an extended spanking program that lasted longer than normal and was performed in front of my grandmother and all the company. Even though my head was a little bumpy and with a little blood on my nose, I received all the attention for the rest of our visit. I'm not sure what happened when we all arrived home, but I do know he never did that again.

13

Explosives and Stuff!

I was walking in a field behind our house one summer afternoon and found a long wire connected to a glass insulator, the kind that are antiques now but back then were mounted on high tension electrical lines. I was going to save the pretty green glass insulator but couldn't get it off the wire, so I started to swing the wire around and around thinking somehow that would loosen it up. As I picked up speed, the combination of the glass insulator and wire made a humming noise, which grew louder and louder the faster I swung the wire. The sound had gotten quite loud when all of a sudden I lost my grip, and the wire and glass insulator went sailing up into the sky headed right for high tension wires! All I could do is stand there as the wire and glass insulator came sailing down from the blue sky and wrapped itself around and around the high tension wires and finally exploded as it shorted itself out. The loud explosion and black smoke detailed the sky as I stood there with my mouth open not believing what just happened. That was first explosion I ever witnessed, and I liked the excitement.

My next excitement happened after a large storm hit our neighborhood and knocked down an old tree in a field behind our house. My mom said it was okay to chop it up for the trash man, so I went to work. As I started to cut off branches, I soon recognized a familiar sight. I had cut off enough branches to form a giant sling shot! I quickly pulled the large sling shot to the side and cleaned up my mess and towed it to the front yard for the trash man.

The next day, I took the sling shot out to the edge of our backyard and dug a hole in the ground and buried the stem of the sling shot deep into the ground. I ran to our pool shed and grabbed and old inner tube that had a hole or two in it, and ran back to my test site. I wrapped the inner tube around the sling shot, and it fit perfectly. We always had weeds growing in our field that looked like little trees, and when you pulled them out of the ground, their root system looked like an arrowhead. I now had my animation for the slingshot. I inventoried a stack of arrowhead weeds, a can of charcoal lighter, matches, and a roll of paper towels and went into the house until night time. After supper, I ran out to my test site and started to wrap a few paper towels around the tip of arrowhead weeds and soaked the towels with charcoal lighter. As I balanced the arrowhead weed on the sling shot and lit the paper towel, a huge flame began to burn, and I launched the flaming arrow high into the air, across the freeway and into the subdivision on the other side. The flaming arrows looked great as they sailed flawlessly into the black sky and then out of site.

At that young age, I never considered what could happen if one of my arrows caught a house on fire or worse! I've also always had a fascination with fireworks. As a young boy, I was introduced to the little explosive tidbits called firecrackers while at a neighbor's house one summer day. He was an older man on our street who had fireworks every year, but I never paid much attention until this particular summer. As a small child, I sometimes heard the explosion on our street and could smell the gun powder, but I was too young to figure out where all the action was taking place. Besides, we weren't allowed to go out of our yard.

This particular summer day was different because I hit the jackpot. While at the neighbor's house, the older man not only let me hold the explosive piece of dynamite, but he said he would light it for me, and I could throw it. You don't know how much those words meant to me at the time. I was in heaven! He was my hero. Nothing else mattered at the time. I had seen similar things explode on TV while watching a fireworks display, and I was about to do the same thing, right here, right now! The countdown was on! The old man pulled a pack of matches from of his faded farmer jeans and ignited the small stick of dynamite. Now it was my turn as tension mounted, and the lit fuse sparkled and spit flames. I threw the ignited firecracker as hard as I could and watched it sail through the air as if there was no gravity. Then with a mighty thunder, the magic cylinder burst in the air, and a million pieces of black and white paper came tumbling down to earth! That was the coolest thing I ever saw in my life.

I immediately ran out to the explosion site and sat down on top of the million pieces of paper, just to examine what just happened! I couldn't believe I just did this! These so-called firecrackers were so very cool. I spent the afternoon at the old man's house just watching and enjoying as these tiny wonders of excitement exploded right in front of me. I loved the thunder and the smell of gun powder, and I never wanted the day to end! As the old firecracker technician exploded each one individually, I noticed he would go into his garage every so often and return with a brand-new pack. I thought at the time maybe it was some kind of firecracker law that restricted you from carrying more than one pack at a time. After his third or fourth trip to the garage, I followed him to see where this ammunition was stored. I saw him open a cabinet door that was about five feet off the ground. Too high for me to reach I thought, as I returned to the test site.

Now that the mystery was solved on where the firecrackers were housed, the day came to an end. I thanked the old man for a great day and peddled my bike back home. As I walked in the house for supper, I reviewed in my mind what had happened that day. I had a lot fun, and I loved the thundering action, but what kept coming back to my head was the cabinet that warehoused the fireworks.

The next day, after a delightful night, dreaming about firecrackers, I rode my bike down to the old man's house again to see more explosions. As I reached his house, I noticed his truck was gone and figured he might be at work. I rang the door bell, but nobody answered. The overhead door was closed and secured, so I went around to the backyard where, just yesterday, all excitement broke loose. I could see no one was in his backyard, so I traveled over to the back door of his garage where the dynamite was stored. To my surprise, the door knob turned and was not locked. Within seconds, I was standing inside the garage, and my heart was beating a hundred miles per hour. I was in the presence of the firecracker cabinet. I looked for a ladder but couldn't find one, not even a stool. I had to reach the top door somehow, some way.

Then it came to me! I'll pull out the white-painted drawer on each level just far enough out to rest my foot on and use the drawers for a ladder to reach the five-foot peak. As I crawled to the top, I looked over my shoulder and noticed it was a long way down, and I was glad the drawers were holding me secure. I finally climbed as far as I could go and was staring at an old faded white cabinet door with grease marks around the handle, but it was the entrance to the fireworks storage. I slowly opened the entrance door, and there they were—layer after layer of sealed black-and-white-colored firecrackers with a mean-looking tiger on the front of each explosive pack. There must have been a gazillion packs of firecrackers in stock!

As my heart was about to explode from beating so hard, I quickly reached in and took a pack, closed the door, scaled back down the partially open drawers I used for a ladder, shut all the drawers to hide any evidence I was ever there, and was out of the garage within seconds. I never pedaled so fast in my life trying to get home and secure the pack if firecrackers without being caught. Once home, I threw my bike down on the driveway and ran into my bedroom. After locking the door and checking both in the closet and under the bed, I was sure at last I was in my safe zone. My heart calmed down, perspiration subsided, and I was finally alone with a whole pack of explosives! I proceeded to my closet and pulled out an old green shoe box I was storing school supplies in. I thought I better secure the firecrackers in the shoe box for safekeeping; after all, I didn't want any explosions in the house. I laid low for the next few days, and nothing was said in the neighborhood about the breaking and entering, so I figured I got away with the heist, and no one would ever know!

The following morning, I planned my day. What would I blow up first? I decided on one of my green army men, so I took the plastic statue and one explosive vessel out of my safe box and headed out to the field behind our house. I placed the green plastic action figure on a hill, piled dirt around the site, and carefully planted the explosive device and was ready for my first experiment. I ignited the fuse with our barbecue matches and ran for cover. I watched as the fuse sparked and smoked and then the explosion. It was spectacular! This was the first time I ignited a firecracker by myself with no adults around. The concussion blew the army man up in the air and almost into space. When the dust and smoke cleared, I ran over to the test site. The concussion blew the army man's head clean off his body. Now that was cool!

I began to blow up soup cans, bugs, glass jars, and my brother's model cars. As I got a little older, I was introduced to bottle rockets from a friend. I wondered why they called them bottle rockets until I investigated a few rockets that had broken sticks, and as I was repairing them, I suddenly saw that they do resemble tiny bottles glued to a stick. I found an old cardboard tube my brother had saved to store parts in, emptied it out, and built a bazooka just like the ones on army shows. I would aim the bazooka at my target, my cousin would load the bottle rocket, tap me on the shoulder to let me know it was loaded, and he was lighting the fuse. Seconds later, the bottle rocket screamed out of the tube and headed for its target. The best advantage point in my neighborhood was on top of my house. I would lean the tip of the bazooka on our chimney for better accuracy and fire away. I could blow up any bicycle that crossed our lawn. The bad news is, you can't always fire accurately because of the wind. I found out the hard way when one of my rockets took a turn for the worst and hit our trampoline and started a small fire.

One summer day, my uncle invited our family to his house for a swim party, so I took numerous bottle rockets with me. When we arrived, he introduced my mom and dad to Tim Conway, the movie star, but I was too young to know who that was, so I went out to set up my rockets. Everyone was having a great time swimming, eating hot dogs and hamburgers on the grill, and enjoying my spectacular aerial rocket show. I loaded a rocket in a Pepsi bottle, lit the fuse, and ran for cover just like I always did. But this time, the wind knocked the bottle over, and the rocket blasted off right over the pool fence and missed my aunt's head by an inch and stuck in the garage before it blew up. She just happened to be sitting next to Tim Conway and jumped up crying and all upset.

Needless to say, I received a pretty hefty spanking and was told to go sit in the car. About thirty minutes later, everyone packed up and went home.

My next adventure as I grew older, wiser, and had a new fireworks contact, was a party in the country. The party consisted of assorted sodas, sandwiches, and fireworks display, all for five dollars. I had a contact from the city and bought a ton of fireworks and took them to my dad's warehouse and started to lay everything out. I used a full sheet of half-inch plywood and used screws and wire to secure every item to the platform. Once that was finished, I ran two packs of five hundred firecrackers all along the edges and topped it off by using a roll of micro fuse to connect every item on the board to one ignition point. I think the platform weighed almost seventy pounds as my friend, and I slowly and carefully loaded it into the van. That night as the sandwiches disappeared and the sun set, it was time to get ready for the grand finally. I had placed the firing platform in the center of a corn field so everyone would be safe, and as I lit the starting fuse, the black cat firecrackers were the first to ignite and echoed thunder, as I ran back to join the audience. The sky was on fire, and the sounds and smells overloaded everyone's senses. The fireworks went on and on, and when the show came to an end, the yard lights came back on, and thick smoke was every where. I think my show lasted longer than the city's display.

My last dealing with fireworks as a young adult was one Christmas when my wife and I visited my brother and his family and purchased a trunk load driving up from Florida. After super, I went out and set up the display in freezing weather and when I was ready, I summoned everyone outside. It was almost a remake of my country fireworks display, but not as long and not the same fireworks used by the city. Everyone cheered and said it was a great show, and it wasn't until years later I found out my brother had just put in a new driveway before the first snow; and when the snow melted, the fireworks had scorched and marred his driveway, which was his pride and joy. That was the last time I fired off any fireworks, but I still miss the excitement.

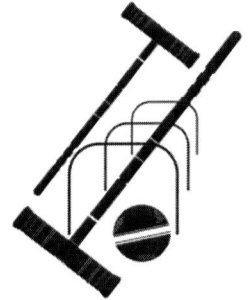

14

Croquet, Anyone?

My brother has always been a car buff. He loved to change oil, install muffler systems, tinker with engines, and customize bodywork. I on the other hand have never changed oil in my life, nor do I ever want to! Car stuff gives me a headache. I remember one summer afternoon, I was trying to find something to do when I found a long chrome pipe in the garage. I think my brother called it a *scavenger pipe*, which in car lingo means a chrome pipe that covers the original tail pipe to make it look cool.

My brother wasn't home, and I knew I could find something to do with this long piece of chrome and quickly grabbed my dad's hammer and went to our backyard. I had a great idea for a home built cannon, so I hammered the chrome scavenger pipe into the soft ground with just a slight angle pointing the tip of the cannon barrel toward the field behind our house. On the far side of the field was the turnpike, and on the other side of the turnpike was a new home development. I knew that was plenty of room for safely firing my new invention. I went back to the garage looking for a projectile but struck out. From there, I traveled to our pool shed located at the edge of our property line. The pool shed was a small white aluminum building, which stored pool supplies like chlorine, pool furniture, and anything else that wouldn't fit in the garage. When I opened the shed screen door, I immediately saw brightly colored croquet balls sitting in a green wooden rack. The croquet balls would be perfect; I hit the jackpot! I grabbed the wooden rack and set it up near my cannon site. Back in those days, you could purchase cherry bombs just like firecrackers and sparklers. Because of the amount of gun powder in a cherry bomb, they were dangerous, and you had to be careful. I happen to have a supply of cherry bombs I was saving for a special day, and today was that day. I pushed a chair into my bedroom closet to reach my shoe box safe on the top shelf. The hidden safe was camouflaged perfectly with an old shirt wrapped around it. I opened the safe and grabbed one cherry bomb and put everything away. I was surprised I had engineered the chrome cannon at such an angle that when I placed a test croquet ball on top, it balanced perfectly.

Now I was ready. I removed the orange stripped croquet ball, ignited the cherry bomb fuse, threw it quickly inside the cannon, balanced the croquet ball on top of the cannon barrel, and ran for cover. It seemed like the fuse burned forever, and then all of a sudden, I heard a huge boom and saw the projectile travel up into the air higher and higher until it looked like a pin dot. I was extremely proud of my first shot that was heard around the neighborhood. The croquet ball seemed to stand still in time, but then I watched as it sailed passed the field, over the turnpike, and headed for the new housing development. I was amazed the projectile traveled so fast and high because I never thought it would get off the ground! As I watched the orange-colored croquet ball fall from the heavens, it suddenly traveled out of site, and I heard a huge thump.

At the time, I assumed it hit the ground, and there would be no reason to stop firing my new creation. I loaded up the next croquet ball and continued firing the chrome cannon until I exhausted my supply of projectiles. It was beginning to get dark outside, so I cleaned up the cannon site, put everything away, and went in the house.

About three weeks later, our whole family was in the station wagon returning home from church where I received a pretty hefty spanking in front of everyone. It just so happened that we went to church on Sunday; other times we went to church on Saturday night, which was the Hispanic service. I think my mom and dad took us to the Saturday service so we could all sleep in the next day. Another interesting fact about that service is that we didn't speak Spanish. The spanking echoed throughout the church, and everyone turned around; so I couldn't start crying, or they would see me. All I was doing is chewing gum, and my dad leaned over and asked me where I got the gum. I told him the truth and said I found it under the pew, and it was Black Jack gum. That's when I was told to spit the gum in his Kleenex and then received the spanking.

On the way home, my dad forgot about the gum incident and mentioned he'd like to play a game of croquet when we got home. He asked my brother and me to set up the game while he was changing his clothes. My brother never noticed that all the balls were missing, and I never said anything. Within a few minutes, we had everything set up and my dad came out to start the game. I'll never forget as he picked up his mallet and went to reach for a ball and there weren't any. I never looked at him while he was throwing a fit and using language that was foreign to me at the time. I just pretended to cry and acted like I didn't know what was going on or where the missing parts were. Needless to say, there was no croquet game that day, and I don't recall if we ever bought new balls to replace the ones that had mysteriously disappeared.

As years went by and my brother and I got older, we did hear a story from our paper boy who moved into that subdivision, about damages occurring to new homes from those croquet balls. I acted surprised just like my brother, but thought to myself how dangerous that day was and how blessed I am that no one was ever injured!

15

Candy Hoist!

My dad designed and built our house as a duplex. My grandma and grandpa lived on one side, and we lived on the other. Next door was my uncle's house and next to him was another uncle. So we had four family homes, side by side. Behind all the homes was a nice big field filled with trees and long grass. I would play army with my youngest cousin, and by late afternoon, we would be pretty dirty and hungry, so we would walk over to my grandma's for a snack. If my mom caught me, I could get in big trouble because she was always telling me not to ruin my appetite for supper.

For some reason when I reached grandma's, she always had a sandwich bag full of peanuts and ready to go. I wished at the time she had a drive up window like the one I saw at the hamburger place so I wouldn't get caught. I made the secret trip to my grandma's food supply a million times, and every time, she would open the squeaky cabinet door, and there was that clear sandwich bag packed to the brim with Spanish peanuts. After squeezing my cheeks and telling me I'm really dirty, she'd hand me the loot, and I would run back and meet my cousin. After bragging about the "mother load," we would race to our fort so my mom wouldn't catch us. Once the coast was clear, we'd pack the red skin peanuts one by one in our mouths until there was no more room. The rule was, you couldn't chew any of the peanuts until the bag was empty. We both looked like a couple of hamsters cramming everything into our cheeks and would always bet who could pack the most in their mouth. It would seem like an hour of chewing once the bag was empty, and we didn't have anything to drink, so our mouths got pretty dry. It's a miracle we didn't choke!

When summer was over, and we went back to school, I was out on the playground one afternoon and saw my grandma walking into church. Our church was across the street from the grade school and our high school, and the candy store was behind both of these buildings. I played private eye and noticed all week my grandma would show up across the street about the same time we had our recess. I decided to wait for her the next day, and when I saw her, I screamed at the top of my lungs, "Hi, grandma!"

She looked over and saw me; as she crossed the street to give me a hug, I had to think fast because I knew she didn't have any peanuts with her. She squeezed my cheeks and gave me the usual hug, and then out of nowhere, I asked her if I could have some money for something to eat. I didn't know where that came from because I already ate lunch, but it worked, and she started digging in her purse. She gave me a quarter, and that's how much our lunch cost, so I knew I had hit the jackpot. I said thanks and ran as fast as I could to the candy store.

The candy store was a place that only a few could go but everybody dreamed about. I had gone into the old gray house, which the school had remolded a few years back and turned it into part storage and part-time candy store. I remember when I first looked inside and saw row after row of dark-stained display cases with miles and miles of candy stacked in neatly organized rows. The smell of candy and sugar filled the air and made me smile without trying. The candy store had everything that you could think of. Penny candy, two for one candy, milk duds, licorice, suckers, good and plenty—you name it, it was behind the glass. Today the aroma was even greater as I walked in the door behind some of the older kids. I began looking at every single item in the candy line up and adding up the cost in my head. When I finally made it up to the candy case with my nose planted securely on the glass, I heard in a loud female squeal, "*Next!*"

It was time for me to order. My voice became squeaky, my palms were sweating, and I couldn't get the words out.

Finally, after I heard, "Can I help you?" out of nowhere, I got the words out, "One Good and Plenty, three black licorices with the red ball in the middle, and five penny candies."

I couldn't believe I just said all that. My head was spinning as I gave the girl my quarter, and in return, the girl folded the top over on a small brown paper bag packed with sugar delights and handed it to me with a smile.

As I walked out of the candy store guarding my treasures, I headed for s safe spot on the playground and started gobbling up the sugar treats. Everything tasted so good I had saliva everywhere, and I never noticed if anyone was watching me slowly emptying the bag. That night, I dreamed what I could buy next week.

Every day, my grandma would arrive just like clock work to attend church, and there I was across the street, yelling, "Hi, grandma," and hinting around for another quarter. I found out later from my dad that after my grandma went to be with the Lord, she had told him the entire story and claimed she always looked forward to each day at the playground.

All that year, I thought I was getting away with it, but my mom and dad knew about it the whole time!

16

Grandma's Lead Foot

Grandma lived next door to us and drove a 1956 Mercury that was in five-star condition. This two-door was built for speed, and Grandma broke it in very well! Since she ran her errands in the morning, sometimes she would take my brother and me to school. We would leave at 7:30 AM and arrive at 7:20 AM, meaning she drove so fast, time went backwards!

One day, coming home from her errands, she catapulted into the driveway a little too fast and hit the side of the garage. Since she was a little hard of hearing, she never heard the screech and crunch of the cold shinny chrome being bent and torn off the light green car, as if it were a slab of butter. My brother and I were delivered home that afternoon via our local school bus, "bus eight the banana crate." I guess because we lived outside the city limits, we inherited bus eight because the city school district didn't want this old shabby bus in town. I remember while riding home, passing the sugar beet company, and gagging on the foul smell, I would dream of someday driving my own car to school so I wouldn't have to put up with the hoodlums who got caught throwing the backseat out the window.

As my brother and I arrived home, we both saw something shiny lying on the garage floor. We ran to see what it was, thinking it could be a new toy or something. Upon arrival, we both began to laugh out loud as hard as we could as we picked up the evidence. Both of us wondered if we were going to get into trouble telling Grandma what she did, and we didn't want to get on her bad side because she always had candy and peanuts. After about five minutes, my brother and I decided not to tell anyone and started to clean up the mess. When we were finished, we both ran into the house to spill the beans on Grandma. I remember Mom and Dad laughing and said they would take care of it but thanked us for cleaning up the mess. I think my dad knew she was a fast driver, and the next day, he showed her the crime seen but all she could say was, "I wonder how that happened."

My dad eventually got the car and garage repaired, but I think we all knew that it could happen again with lead foot behind the wheel. My brother eventually purchased the green two-door and since he was a car enthusiast, began to tweak the engine, exhaust, and made other changes. As time went on and he was working his magic, the car began to take on a whole new look. It changed from Grandma's car to a high speed dragster. It was always a fast car, but now it was faster and had a new sound and a new look. My brother kept the car super clean both inside and out.

At my young age, I didn't have a car nor did I want one. The only thing I wanted was to borrow twelve dollars from my friends to purchase a pair of "Beatle" boots, which was the craze after the group landed in the United States. I walked home the day I bought the boots, and I thought I was really cool. I skipped a lot of lunches to pay back my friends but eventually got everyone paid. I took two of the silver tabs under the kitchen chairs that keep the chair from scratching the floor and pounded one in each of my boots, so now you could really hear the heal of my boot every time I walked.

As I grew out of the boots and eventually got older, I purchased my brother's car, but I was the exact opposite. I knew where to put the gas in, but that was about it! I remember the glorious day when my parents said I was responsible enough to drive to school, but there were to be no passengers and to drive straight to school and straight home. That sounded fair enough. Finally, the first school morning arrived as I fired up the two-door and proceeded to school. Upon arriving at the parking lot, I couldn't help but to reeve the engine so everyone knew I had arrived. It worked, and all my friends ran over to look at my new ride. I remember all day long, whenever I passed a window, I would look out to see my green two-door just waiting for me to get out of class and drive it home.

As the days and weeks went by, I became more and more comfortable with my new car. One afternoon, I was leaving the high school parking lot, and two freshmen girls across the street were checking me out. I had the windows down pretending I was listening to the radio when I heard one of them yell out something. I cruised over to see what they wanted and my heart began to beat fast and my hands started to sweat.

The girls said they liked my car and wanted to know if I could give them a ride to the bus stop.

"Sure," I said, as I opened the door so both of them could sit up front with me.

I guess with the short skirts and the friendly smiles sitting beside me, I completely forgot about the "no passenger" clause my folks advised me of. As I drove the most populated streets to the girl's bus stop, I made sure everyone I knew noticed my car with not one but two girls in the front seat with me. As I slowly came to a stop to let my passengers out, I happened to glance in the rearview mirror and saw my mom two inches from my back bumper, in her station wagon, pointing her finger at me. I instantly got chills down my back and thought to myself, *How did she find me? What is she doing here?* I was so busy thinking about how much trouble I was in, I never heard what the girls were saying as they got of the car. When I returned home, the ever so popular yelling and screaming began, and the car was grounded for the next month.

The next school day was the most embarrassing because I arrived at school on bus eight the banana crate. I had to explain something to my friends, so I told them the truth and explained my brother was rebuilding the engine, and the project would take about a month. I saved some dignity that day but never saw those two girls again. I learned my lesson and drove straight home the rest of the school year.

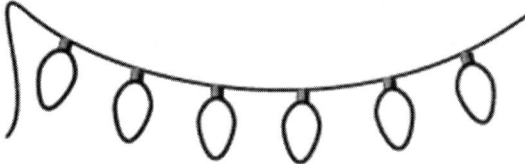

17

Christmas Lights

One of my uncles lived two doors down from our house. He was the first one in our neighborhood to own a snow blower, and that was a big deal. One Christmas season, we had an overwhelming snowfall, and my uncle cleared off his driveway and made a mile high mountain of compact snow. My cousin and I watched him most of the day, clearing his walks and driveway, and it seemed like as soon as he finished one section, the heavy snow filled it back up. The snow flurries were huge, and while we were playing and watching my uncle working, we tried to catch the flakes in our mouth as they filled the sky in slow motion.

Later that afternoon, the snow slowed down, and my uncle was covered in white and was soaking wet as he traveled back into his house for the rest of the day. He had the only cleared walks and driveway in the neighborhood. My cousin and I walked down to examine the snow my uncle had blown into a huge mountain from all his work that day. It was huge. It had to have been six or seven feet tall and was packed solid. After a few minutes of awe, I told my cousin we should make a fort out of this huge white mountain and with his mouth wide open screamed cool! We quickly drew our blueprint in the snow and ran back to our houses to get all the supplies we needed to start construction. As the clock ticked patiently, both of us were back and ready to start work within fifteen minutes. We had to work fast because the daylight would soon be gone, and it seemed like it was getting colder. I examined the mountain of snow and decided to put the door facing the street lights. As we carved out the entrance, my cousin and I were careful to pull the door section out all in one piece. After laying aside the door, we began to hollow out the inside, shovel after shovel. Soon I was able to crawl inside and shovel snow into a cardboard box we brought our supplies in, slide it out the door; and it was my cousin's job to empty the box all around the sides of the mountain, covering our previous footprints. It seemed like we were working for hours, but then the moment of glory came, and we had our room carved out. We both were inside, all cozy. And believe it or not, it seemed to be warmer inside our fort. We had only a few things to take care of before we traveled back home for supper. We took the round handle end of the shovel and poked a small hole through the wall of the fort facing my uncle's house. Next, we went out side and shaved down the door thickness so it wouldn't be so heavy and then poked a hole through the middle of the door. Next, we fed one end of a swing set rope through the hole, tied a big knot, and packed snow around the knot so you couldn't see it. Now we had a way to pull the door closed once we were inside.

 As the day ended, we gathered our tools and agreed to meet back at the fort in an hour, and I would bring a surprise. My cousin was excited as we sealed the camouflaged entrance door and ran home for supper. As I gobbled my food down, it tasted good and warmed me up for phase two that night. After supper, I ran to the basement and grabbed my dad's BB gun, wrapped it in a bath towel, slid it through the basement window, put the box of ammo in my pocket, and headed outside. It seemed like it was getting much colder as I grabbed the secret package and ran to the snow fort.

Darkness arrived, and the street lights could be seen in between the snowflakes. Minutes later, my cousin arrived as I pulled the entrance door back, and we both got inside quickly and pulled the door closed behind us. I brought a candle from our dinning room table, and my cousin brought his dad's Zippo lighter, and soon we had all the light I needed to bring out the wrapped surprise. As I unwrapped the BB gun from the bath towel, my cousin's eyes lit up, and he asked what we were going to do with a BB gun. Under the soft flicker of the candle, I loaded the weapon barrel one at a time with the brass-colored ammunition, and the excitement was so thick you could cut it with a knife! I explained to my cousin that my uncle's Christmas lights had been on for several hours, and when the lights are hot, they pop loud when they break. He looked a little confused as he watched. I slid the barrel of the weapon out the small hole we punched through earlier, facing the house, and with careful aim, fired the first round hitting the light dead center only to hear a crisp tiny explosion and the sound of glass shattering. My cousin's smile was from ear to ear as he said wow about a hundred times.

For my next shot, I picked out a shinny red bulb and slowly pulled the trigger only to hear the shattering glass once again. It was so cool to watch as the glass exploded into a million pieces, and a small puff of smoke raced into the cold night air. I fired shot after shot as each bulb sputtered, and the shattering noise echoed the cold crisp night. I was pretty proud of hitting each one of my tiny targets, but then my cousin asked if he could shoot the gun. I hesitated but then thought, after all, he did help with the construction of the fort. He slid the gun barrel out the tiny hole, and I told him to take careful aim and squeeze the trigger slowly. I watched intensely as he picked out the bright blue bulb and pulled the trigger. I was waiting to hear the glass breaking, and the little puff of smoke released into the night air; but instead, I heard it ricochet off my uncle's picture window and hit his front door. Suddenly within seconds, the front porch light came on, and I heard the front door unlocking. I quickly pulled the gun back inside, blew out the candle, and told my cousin to be quiet and sit still.

As I peered out and saw my uncle coming down his freshly shoveled steps, he headed toward the fort. I quickly sat back and watched as he walked past so close I could see his pajamas and robe within inches of the gun barrel access hole. My heart was beating fast, my hands were sweating, and my cousin looked like he was going to pass out, as my uncle looked at all the Christmas lights that had been broken. He walked back and forth three or four times looking at his lights and then looking out at the street. It seemed like I was holding my breath for an hour when finally I watched as he headed back to the front door. The lights went off, the locks locked, and everything was quiet. I saw the curtain move, so I knew we had to sit still for a few more minutes while my uncle took his last look.

It seemed like forever, but finally, everything settled down. You could hear the street lights humming and the wind sailing past the fort as drifts were magically appearing everywhere. All this time, my cousin and I never said a word as I finally whispered, "Let's get out of here." We pushed the entrance door open, gathered all our supplies, crawled out of the fort slowly, and made sure we kept close to the ground. As we pushed the door closed and covered our footprints with a small branch from my uncle's shrub, I told my cousin I would see him tomorrow morning and told him not to say a word about what happened tonight to anybody. He agreed, and we walked home through the white snow drifts in dead silence.

The next morning, I called my cousin and told him I would be at his house in ten minutes. He agreed and assured me he never mentioned anything to anyone. During our top secret conference meeting, my cousin and I agreed we both had a close call and would not travel back to the crime seen until summer arrived. My uncle never did find out what happened but told our dads he had over a dozen broken Christmas lights and thought we should all be on the look out to help keep vandalism off our street!

18

Kidnapping

My aunt and uncle lived two houses down from our house and had a dog named Scottie. Scottie was very friendly and was always in the backyard except at night when he was aloud indoors. One day, I was outside playing with my cousin, and we saw Scottie leisurely walking down the street. We called his name, and he stopped sniffing the ground and came running to us right away. My cousin and I petted Scottie, and he licked our hands as we headed for my aunt and uncle's house. As I rang the doorbell, Scottie sat down and looked at us like he was trying to say thank you for bringing me home. He was a good dog and minded very well.

My aunt answered the door dressed in her cleaning clothes as we explained the situation, and she replied that Scottie had been getting out when the gate was left open and concluded her daughter may have left it open. She invited my cousin and me to step inside and to our surprise behind the door, was a huge bowel filled to the top with jaw breakers. Each of the brightly colored individually wrapped jaw breakers were piled high in the biggest bowel I had ever seen. The bowel was big enough to give Scottie a bath in and then have room left over. My aunt politely said help yourselves for bringing Scottie back safe and sound. I happened to look over at my cousin, and his eyes were bulging out of his head, wandering how someone could have that many jawbreakers. Both of us reached over and took one jawbreaker each. We both picked blue, which stains your tongue while the candy is dissolving. That night, before falling asleep, I was thinking about that spectacular bowel of candy and suddenly realized how my cousin and I could get more jawbreakers!

The next day, I was so excited I couldn't wait for my cousin to wake up. I discussed the plan of attack and made sure he understood his role as we proceeded to my aunt and uncle's house. As we arrived at the big cedar tree at the edge of their property, we proceeded to lie on the ground so no one could see us and examine the backyard where Scottie was playing. Scottie had an old tennis ball he played with and always wanted someone to throw it. It was a gross ball full of grass stains, dirt, and always had a gallon of saliva that would drip off and get on your hand just before you throw the ball. We ran over to the gate and called Scottie, and he proceeded to run to us with that stinky ball in his mouth. I think Scottie thought we were calling him over to throw the ball. I proceeded to open the gate and called Scottie to follow me, and he was all excited and followed us around the house and to the front porch.

We rang the doorbell and hoped someone was home. We waited for some time, and no one came to the door, so I rang it again. This time my aunt came to the door, out of breath and explained she was in the basement, and then realized we had Scottie once again. My cousin and I were invited in and took advantage of the overwhelming bowl and this time grabbed a handful of jawbreakers. The dog kidnapping went on for almost a week until one day we were on our way to kidnap again, and as we turned the corner by the cedar tree, I saw my uncle in his backyard. We both slammed on the brakes and hit the ground so he wouldn't see us. The limbs of the cedar tree provide ample camouflage as we lay under the limbs and watched my uncle walking foot by foot along the fence. He was talking to himself, but we couldn't hear what he was saying. My cousin and I decided that day, the delicious jawbreakers were all finished.

We found out later that my aunt told my uncle to search the backyard for the escape route, and their daughter got a spanking for leaving the gate open.

19

Bat Attack

When my brother and I were in grade school, every so often my mom and dad would leave us at grandma's house while they went on vacation. The last time my brother and I were on vacation with my mom and dad, we were traveling in our new station wagon with the fake wood siding, and we stopped at a restaurant to eat. When leaving, I was the last one to slide out of the booth and saw money my dad left lying by his plate. I figured he forgot it, so I picked it up and put it in my pocket to give to him when we were back in the car.

After traveling for about fifteen minutes, I remembered the money and pulled it out and told my dad he left his money at the restaurant. He slammed on the brakes to give me a spanking and then as he turned the car around to head back to the restaurant and explained that was the girl's tip. My grandma's house was well within walking distance to our grade school, so my brother and I would always arrive early to play on the merry-go-round until the bell rang.

I remember when the very first vending machine arrived at our grade school, and I used to dream about it all the time and wish I could purchase something. The machine had brand-new pencils and pads of paper and pens and all kinds of school supplies, and everything cost a quarter, which was the same as our lunch. I guess they made the price the same as our lunch, so if you ran out of paper or pencils, you could purchase them instead. I remember not paying attention to the teacher because I was busy tracing things on the back of my pad, when all of a sudden, I had an idea. Why not trace a quarter, cut it out with a scissors, and use the cardboard plug in the vending machine? Could that really work? I hurried and traced the quarter I had for lunch and had to be quick because the recess bell was about to ring; and as my hands began to sweat, I maneuvered the pencil around the quarter, making sure to keep the circle perfect. Finally, my masterpiece was traced, cut out, and ready for the machine. Just then, the bell rang, and as I traveled to my locker, I swung around and put the masterpiece in the coin slot, pulled the lever, and a brand-new pack of paper came out at the bottom, and I ran to put it in my locker. I thought that was so cool and always hoped the school would get more vending machines.

My grandma was very strict with us while staying at her house, and she would make us go to bed exactly on time, every day, including the weekends. We weren't allowed to turn on very many lights, so the house was always creepy at night. After any meal, you were not permitted to eat anything until the next meal; and after supper, you didn't eat anything until the next day. My brother and I got smart and made up a story about needing money every day for school and my grandma thought it was for our lunch. Little did she know, my mom had already given us our lunch money. My grandma's donation was going to a good cause. My brother and I passed a grocery store every day on the way to school, and this cash would be spent on snacks. Every day we would purchase hostess cupcakes or candy or potato chips to smuggle back to Grandma's house to eat in our bedroom at our leisure.

One night after our snack buffet, we were getting ready for bed, and my brother told me I had a brown mark on the back of my underwear. Instead of pulling my pants down and looking, or at least looking in a mirror, I ran downstairs and pushed my bottom on my grandma's leg and asked her if I had a brown mark on my underpants. At the time, Grandma was relaxing and calmly reading the paper. As she looked up over the top of her reading glasses, she yelled no and went back to reading. I ran back up stairs and told my brother what happened, and he just laughed and said, "I know, I just wanted to see if you would do it."

I kept the underpants on since it was my last pair, and we were going home in the morning. As night time arrived, and our stomachs were filled with our smorgasbord of snacks, we both fell asleep, and I dreamed about traveling home the next day. About two o'clock in the morning, I remember hearing a monotone voice, but I couldn't understand it. I heard the same thing over and over again. It was kind of a muffle noise. As I started to wake up and clear my eyes, I realized it was my brother screaming under his covers, "Bat attack, bat attack!"

As I peeked over my blanket, I could hear and see this black bird flying at great speeds at the top of our ceiling in the bedroom. At first I thought it was cool, but then it started to swoop down at my blanket due to my movement. I instantly crawled under my covers like my brother, but I could still hear the thing flying. I yelled to my brother and asked him, "Why is a bird in our bedroom?"

He yelled back, "It's a bat, not a bird."

I don't remember how long we both lay perfectly still with our covers over our head so the bat would think we were gone.

I fell back asleep, and before I knew it, morning had come, and the bat was nowhere in site. We found out at breakfast when we told the scary story to Grandma that it was indeed a bat, and she more or less boasted she gets them all the time in her house. My brother and I never did like that house because of the bats, but when I grew up and my grandmother passed away, I bought the house. Next door to Grandma's house was a greenhouse, which years before a family started the flower business out of their house and eventually built glass walls and roof, and I could look out the windows in my house and look at all the inventory. I remember one Saturday night when I first moved in and I was putting things away, I unpacked my dad's old BB gun. I decided to load it up with ammo and bring back some old memories. I always wanted to turn a light on and shoot a bulb out so I could watch it spark and spit and then go out, so I aimed for a small bulb in the chandelier and fired a round. The BB missed the bulb, bounced off the wall, and landed on the floor some place. I took careful aim and fired the second round, and with spectacular accuracy, the BB hit the bulb dead center breaking it into a million pieces. You could literally hear and see the spark and sputter of the bulb as it slowly went out. I could now mark this bit of craftsmanship off my bucketlist and ready myself for what will happen next.

I assumed it was late enough; I slowly opened the window facing the greenhouse so I could fire another round. I aimed carefully at one of the greenhouse windows and slowly pulled the trigger. Since window glass is thicker than light bulb glass, I assumed the projected BB would bounce off the window just like it did on the wall, but to my surprise, the pane of glass broke into several reflective pieces and fell to the ground. In the dead of night, it seemed like the sound of the breaking glass was magnified as I quickly shut the window and turned the lights off to see if anyone heard the echoing sounds. I waited for quite some time, but no lights turned on in the greenhouse, so I put the BB gun away and finished putting my things away. The next day,

I never went near the window of the crime scene; but three days later, I glanced out at night and noticed the mess was cleaned up, and a new pane of glass was installed. Years later, the business was sold and the greenhouse torn down and is a vacant lot to this day.

20

Best Easter Ever

One Easter, my brother and I received a baby chick from a friend, and we were ecstatic! This was our first pet ever, and we got to keep it in the basement. I remember it like it was yesterday. We were so excited with the new edition we even painted a cardboard box with shutters on the windows and a fake front door. We would travel to the basement and play for hours. The yellow chick was so small that if you held it in one hand, he would almost disappear. The one problem my brother and I had was when it was time to go back upstairs and the lights went out, the chick would get scared and start chirping up a storm. We figured out if we left a small light on, the chick thought we were still there, and the chirping would stop. We planned on playing with the chick the next day, so we both went upstairs to watch TV.

The next morning was Easter, and my brother and I woke up early excited to find colorful Easter eggs, jelly beans, and chocolate treats of all sizes. My brother told me it was too early to wake everybody up, so we decided to bring the baby chick from his freshly painted house and play with it in our bedroom. I was elected to travel to the basement, so I put on my Roy Rogers slippers and ran to the basement to retrieve our guest. I held the chick in both hands as I slowly approached the linoleum-covered steps. The basement was an okay place if the lights were on, but at night was when the boogie man came out. I remember one time when my brother and I were laughing late one night, and my mom heard my voice and was upset with me and made me go to the basement to sleep on an old outside lounge chair. Halfway down the steps she turned the lights out and I had to run for the chair before the boogie man saw where I was. With no blanket to hide under, I kept my eyes shut tight and finally went to sleep, but the next morning, I ran upstairs where it was safe. Thinking about that story, I was hoping the chick was quiet as I reached the top of the stairs and proceeded to our bedroom where my brother was waiting patiently. Now that we were all safe and nothing could go wrong, we started to play with our new friend. We had a blast with the chick making pillow forts and letting him run wild on the floor, but I think his favorite place was under the sheets. We decided to see if he would run in a straight line, so we cleared an area on the floor and marked each end of the carpet with a piece of scotch tape for the start and finish lines. My brother bet me that the chick would run farther when it was his turn. I told him the bet was on, and we started the contest.

My brother was first up, and when he let the chick go, all you saw was a yellow streak go by, and my brother was yelling and getting excited and woke my dad up. We heard his bedroom door open, and I grabbed the chick, and my brother and I both jumped in our beds at the same time. The little chick ran under my sheet and never made a peep as my dad entered the room all upset. He was yelling about us waking everybody up, and it was early so we better get back to sleep, or there would be no Easter for us. We said okay, and he walked out and slammed the door. You could have heard a pin drop as we lay quiet for what seemed like an hour when all of a sudden, I could hear my brother laughing under his covers.

I looked over and whispered, *"Why are you laughing?"*

He told me to look at the floor where we set up the running track for the chick. As I looked over, I started to laugh too. My brother and I didn't notice that when the chick was warming up for the marathon, he deposited brown runny poop trails all down the carpet, and when my dad came in, he stepped right on the brown slush with his bare feet. My brother must have scared the little chick when he started yelling as he ran toward the finish line. That was so funny to look at, but what was even funnier was my dad's footprint that left our bedroom and back into my mom and dad's bedroom. The liquid slush was a clear sign we had to get the chick back into the basement before everyone got up. It was my brother's turn, so he loaded the chick up in the pocket of his blue robe and headed for the basement. He deposited the chick back into his cardboard castle and on the way back grabbed the kitchen towel, got it wet, and headed to our bedroom. The coast was clear, and we took turns wiping up the smashed poop on the carpet. We finally finished cleaning the carpet, except for the smell, and got back in bed and went to sleep.

About two hours later, we heard my sisters were up and knew it was time for the egg hunt. We had a great day playing with our chick and finding a lot of Easter eggs and candy, but the bad news was my dad said we had to give the chick away. My brother and I were sad, but we had lots of eggs and candy to make us happy again. I don't know if my dad ever found out about the crushed poop on the bottom of his foot, but we never said a word. The paperboy took our chick into his homemade house and lived happily ever after, and for my brother and I, we had the best Easter ever!

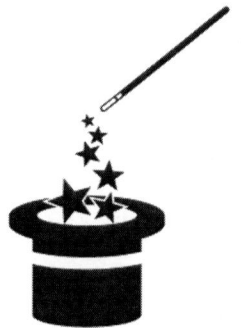

21

Street Magic

Sometimes you run out of things to do, growing up on a dead-end street. It was always the same kids, the same houses, and hot summer days. I had just finished polishing my dad's shoes and backing them into his closet with the black shoes first and then the brown shoes and then finally his slippers. He didn't ask me to polish them; I just thought it was a nice idea. I was bored and had an idea to set up a magic show. I always loved magic and watched it on TV any time I could. Magic was always cool because now you see it, say a magic word, and presto—it was gone.

Whenever we went to the hobby shop, I always looked for a magic item I could afford and then rushed home to play with it and then put it in my collection. I scrambled to the front yard to search for the best tree that was close to the road but large enough for kids to get under the branches. I found the perfect tree and ran into the house to drag my bedspread out to the stage area and used my mom's clothes pins to attach it to different branches making it look like a dome. After careful planning and precise areas to pin my rainbow-colored bedspread to tree limbs, the colorful and magical dome was complete.

Now I had to transfer pool furniture for seating, and the best way for trucking these auditorium seats to the stage area was with my trusty red wagon. I traveled around the house, moved a big rock by the fence to get the key to unlock the pool gate, and pulled my wagon into the loading zone. This was the same pool I was caught peeing in when it was brand-new. The man with the water truck was filling up the pool, and my brother and I were acting like we were swimming. The water was only waste high at the time, and I was swimming the backstroke when all of a sudden I got the urge to go to the bathroom. I let it out slowly thinking no one would know. Just then, the waterman came over to where I was standing and dipped some type of gauge into the water and slowly walked over to my dad; both of them were talking and looking at me. Then my dad asked me if I went number one in the pool and right away I said no and he told me to get out of the pool. I acted like I didn't do anything and ran into the house. As I backed my wagon into position, the first chairs closest to me were the twin white plastic chairs that looked like they needed a bath due to dirt and grime built up from the winter.

Next were three of the multicolored cloth strap chairs. These were my favorite because they didn't get hot when you sat on them with a wet bathing suit. Last, I needed a table to perform all my magic tricks, and the stool matching the chairs would work out perfect. I carefully trucked my load to the front yard and started to unload inside the dome.

Once I finished, I preceded into the house to custom make the admission tickets. I had a blue shoe box in my bedroom and started to cut squares from the sides and top of the box, and when finished, I used a black crayon to print each ticket exactly the same. I wanted the kids to think I had the tickets printed up someplace. I made sure the word *magic* was in large print and also drew a glass of lemonade and printed at the bottom, "all for twenty five cents." I parked my bike and the red wagon on the side of the dome, so it looked like kids were already saving their seats. I think it took about a half hour for the first neighborhood kid to arrive, and I told him to go get everyone he knew for free lemonade. He was pretty excited and took off on his bike to tell the rest of the neighborhood. It wasn't long before the Vegas style dome was a packed house.

I didn't have anything magical to wear to make me look like a magician, so I kept my eyes wide open and stared at everyone like the magicians do on TV. Some of the kids asked why I was staring, but I acted like I didn't hear them. After collecting the admission fee and serving lemonade, the "Great Haroldeanie" proceeded with the show, and everyone seemed to be enjoying themselves. All I heard that afternoon was, "That was cool," and, "How did you do that?" Along with seeing everyone's mouth hanging open and the refreshments gone, it was time to dismiss the patrons because it was almost suppertime. The show was a lot of work setting up, and it was over in no time. I couldn't leave the stage up because I needed my bedspread and because everyone in the neighborhood saw the show. I dismantled the Vegas dome and hauled the pool furniture back in place just in time for supper. I think I made about two dollars and twenty five cents that day and saved it in my bank for the next visit to the hobby shop.

22

Christmas Time

Christmas at my house was a little different than most homes, only I never realized it at the time. My mom would have us kids get the silver Christmas tree out of the basement and start putting it together on Christmas Eve. It was quite evident we always waited to the last minute for everything, and I always wondered why we never got a real tree. I guess the silver tree was okay, but you get tired real fast of watching the spinning disc changing colors from green to red to orange to blue and back to green again. I guess all those colors shining on the tree were supposed to make you think the tree was real, or maybe get you in the Christmas spirit. That was the only Christmas decoration we ever put up in our house, and since we didn't hang ornaments or bulbs or angle hair on the tree, the whole escapade took about twenty minutes and then another ten minutes to put our gifts for others under the tree, and we were finished.

The next step was to watch TV and then go to bed. That was our typical Christmas Eve schedule. The next day was Christmas morning, and whatever time we wake up, we had to wait until everyone was out of bed and then we could open up our presents. When we all arrived in the living room, we noticed there were more gifts under the tree, and my mom always explained that Santa came right after we went to bed. That was another thing I always wondered about. Why did we always have to go to bed early? Why not stay up just a little longer so we could see Santa?

After opening up our gifts and receiving the new book bag, underwear, socks, and maybe one or two presents we really wanted, it was time to take the tree down, unplug the spinning light, and store everything back in the basement.

Christmas at our house was usually over around nine o'clock in the morning, and we were told to put away our presents and wash up for breakfast. This opulent Christmas story happened year after year until finally, one year I broke the mystery and solved the questions I always wondered about. It happened early one December morning as I woke up and started walking down the hallway to get some Kellogg's frosted flakes, when all of a sudden, I could hear my mom and dad talking about her hiding the presents in the same place she did last year. I stopped in my tracks so no one could see or hear me and listened intently for more valuable information like, what presents? How many? Where were they hidden? But that information was never divulged. I was on my own now and had a mission.

I was excited but nervous that I may get caught during this investigation, so timing was everything! I waited day after day for the right time and then finally got a break. My mom and dad were going to a bingo, my brother was out of the house with his friend, and my sisters were staying overnight for a sleepover. I knew what time my brother would be back because he was supposed to be watching me, so I had to act fast. Once the coast was clear, I started my search. I moved every dusty item in the attic and then put it right back in the same spot so no one knew I was there. I searched my brother's bedroom from top to bottom, no luck! Next, I went to my sister's bedrooms and did the same thing. So far, nothing but a bunch of underwear and books. As the sweat dripped from my forehead, I moved quickly into my mom and dad's bedroom and started the investigation all over again. Once more, I found nothing that could be used for Christmas gifts.

The final resting place for my search would be the basement. I was down there a million times but never saw anything that looked like hidden presents, but I had to find the treasure, and this was the only room left! I pressed forward and started the search. I checked the bathroom, no luck. I searched the vacant rooms, no luck. The only area left was the piano room where my dad listened to our piano lessons on Saturday and advised my brother and me what we were doing wrong and what he expected on the next lesson. I searched the shelving and boxes opposite the piano with no luck. As I sat down on the cedar chest scratching my head and thinking there are no more rooms, I suddenly looked at what I was sitting on and remembered I never looked inside this chest. I tried the latch, but it was locked. I ran out to the garage and grabbed a hammer and a screwdriver and carefully went to work. I tried to pick the lock with the screwdriver, but that only works in the movies. I tapped the screwdriver several times with the hammer, which forced the lock into the chest splitting the wood. At last I could finally open the lid, and when I looked inside, I found the treasure I'd been searching for!

Wrapped presents were neatly stacked high with our names on them just waiting to be handed out on Christmas day. I carefully memorized how they were stacked as I took out the gifts one at a time. When I came to a gift that had my name on it, I would stop, use one of my dad's double-sided blades from his razor, and carefully slice the scotch tape on one end of the gift, slide the present out, and examine what I would be getting for Christmas. When I was finished, I wrapped the gift back up and put a new piece of scotch tape on top of the old sliced tape and put it back on the pile. I went all the way to the bottom of the cedar chest pulling out and examining every one of my gifts and putting them back exactly where I found them so no one would ever know I was there. I was so proud I found the treasure, looked at all my gifts, and put everything back the way it was without anyone finding out.

As the days went by, everyone knew Christmas was almost here, and it was time to get the silver Christmas tree from the basement and get it set up. My brother and I were busy pulling the silver tree limbs out of the paper covers and inserting them in the tree base when we heard my mom calling us to the basement. It wasn't a sweet call like we did something nice; it was a "get down here before you both get a spanking" call. As I traveled swiftly down the basement steps, sometimes skipping a step, I suddenly remembered the cedar chest and hammer episode. I had completely forgotten about hitting the lock on the cedar chest so many times I broke the wood around the lock, and now my mom had found the crime scene. By this time, I was down the basement steps and standing in the piano room with my brother. My mom, all red-faced and looking totally upset, was holding a piece of broken wood from the cedar chest in her hand and ready to kill somebody. I knew right then I would have to bite the bullet and let her know that I broke the cedar chest because I didn't have time to come up with a story. I told her I couldn't get the lid to open and thought it was stuck and used a hammer and accidently broke it. I received a spanking when my dad got home that night, was grounded for two weeks, and told never to touch that cedar chest again. I took the punishment and never told them about the presents and scotch tape, and believe it or not, my mom continued to hide the gifts in the same place for years.

23

Escaping Nap Time

I can remember as a small child how fascinated I was with the mail. I was too young to read, but I loved to put the different envelope sizes and colors in order. I saw my dad's office one time, and he had a large desk with only about ten inches of work space. He had all kinds of letters and mail and paperwork stacked up all over the place, and I thought he was so lucky to have all those treasures on top of his desk. I didn't know what all the paperwork was, but it was a masterpiece to me. I would wait for the mailman to arrive on our street, and as soon as he drove away, I ran out to bring the contents into the house. I would find my mom right away so she could go through everything and give me my mail, which at the time was all the resident mail, but I thought it had my name on it. I rushed to my bedroom and got out my shoe box, which I thought was my briefcase, and put all the new mail

I received in order. I had the shoe box filled almost to the top, and some days I would dump everything out on the carpet and go through each letter page by page and then file it back in color, order, and size. I finished packing the mail in my briefcase and was outside playing army with all the neighborhood kids when I heard my mom calling my brother and me. The awful call would materialize every afternoon, and my brother and I knew what it was all about. We had to go inside and take a nap. We hated to take a nap because after you woke up, all the kids were gone, and everything was over.

As we walked the slow dreaded funeral walk into the house and all the other kids proceeded to play, we headed for our bedrooms. My brother and I had hooked up toy telephones from his bedroom to my bedroom years ago, and we would talk back and forth at night so my mom and dad couldn't hear us. As I lie in bed thinking about this nap time incident, I came up with a brain storm and called my brother. I told him I would wait about twenty minutes and then rub my cheeks on the carpet until they were red to make it look like I was sleeping. Then I would go out and tell my mom I just woke up, and I'm going outside to go play. If my mom fell for it, I would travel back into the bathroom, which was between our bedrooms, and drop the plastic drink cup in the sink, which was the signal I made it out. He was to wait about ten minutes and then rub his cheeks on the carpet, and I'd meet him outside. I hung up the toy phone and proceeded to rub my cheeks on the carpet and headed out to find my Mom. After checking several rooms, I found her in the living room enjoying a cup of coffee and reading the newspaper and gave her my spiel, and she fell for it hook, line and sinker. She said I could go play but not to make a lot of noise so I wouldn't wake up my brother. As soon as I was out of the living room, I ran like the wind back to the bathroom, dropped the drinking cup in the sink, and ran outside to get back with the neighborhood kids.

About twenty minutes after my return, my brother showed up with a grin from ear to ear because our secret assignment worked. We played the rest of the day, and as the weekend came to an end, we went back to school on Monday, and I decided to take my briefcase to show my classmates my exciting collection. I couldn't believe the remarks and attitude I was getting at school as I proudly displayed my brilliant work for everyone to see. No one seemed to care or knew what it was. I just figured they were jealous and went on with my day guarding my life's work until I got home.

The next day, I was back in school, and everything was going well until I came home that afternoon, and I couldn't find my briefcase. I looked under my bed, in my secret hiding place, and all over the house. It was time to start crying, but I thought I would ask my mom first if she saw it in the house. She said she was cleaning and found an old shoe box with scraps of paper and envelopes and pitched in the trash being picked up that morning. I forgot when I came home the night before, I left my briefcase in the living room, and that's where my mom found it. She had no idea it had all my treasures and hard work. I cried for a long time that night, and my mom said she was sorry, but somehow that didn't help me, and I never forgot all the work I put into my collection.

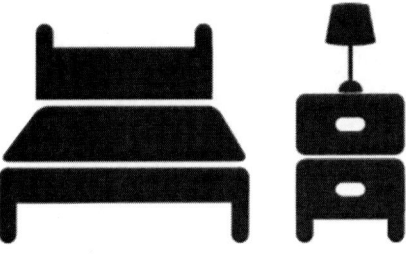

24

New Bedrooms

One year, my mom and dad decided to remodel a section of our house and advised my brother and me that we were going to get our own bedrooms. We were excited until we found out there was good news and bad news. The good news was, we were getting brand-new colorful modern bedrooms. The bad news was, these so-called new bedrooms were going to be in the basement. My mom assured us there was nothing to fear in the basement, everything would be new, and we were to take good care of our new rooms.

During construction, the carpenters worked hard and built cabinets to store our toys and books in, installed new desks, which we never had before, laid new carpet, installed new ceilings, and completed the job with new paint. In the old basement, you always heard noises you never knew where they were coming from; the lighting was so poor you couldn't see where the monsters were hiding, and odors you couldn't identify.

Now all that was gone, and the smell of "new" filled my senses. The new lighting made me think I was outside, and the soft carpet made me feel cozy and warm, and my built-in desk made me want to do my homework!

One day after the construction was completed and my brother and I were moved into our new bedrooms, we were playing a board game; and when it was over, my brother went to his bedroom to do his homework. I put everything away in my new cabinets and went to my brother's bedroom and started teasing him about me winning. He got upset and told me to get out of his bedroom. I continued until he got real mad, and as I was running out of his bedroom, he threw his Bic pen at me, and somehow it stuck momentarily in the back of my head as I fell on the floor like I was dead. The pen fell out when I hit the floor, and it hurt a little bit but looked far worse than what it was. Sitting at his desk and staring at me, he kept saying over and over, "I know you're not dead."

It seemed like forever as I lay on the floor, concentrating on how I was breathing so my stomach wouldn't move. Again he said, "I know you're not dead."

Finally after about twenty minutes, he came over and tickled me to see if I would move. I couldn't hold it in any longer and busted up laughing, in fact, I laughed so hard tears were forming on my face.

I know I scared my brother, but all he said was, "I told you. You weren't dead." And he traveled back to his bedroom!

Later that afternoon, I called my cousin who lived next door, to travel over and see my new bedroom. My cousin knew we were getting remolding done and always wanted to hang around and was excited to see the finished project. As soon as I hung up, I didn't even get up the basement steps and heard the door bell ring. It was a lugubrious day and had been snowing, and my cousin was bored and just about to come over anyway when I placed the call. He told me he was there for the "bedroom inspection" as I invited him in and advised him to take his shoes off. He had a smile on his face as he came down the steps and saw the colorful improvements. He loved my bedroom and said he wanted to stay there forever. We talked for awhile and decided to get my new chemistry kit out I received for Christmas the previous year. The shiny red metal case with chrome handles and two doors had a picture of a scientist on the front working on an experiment. Once the three red latches were unlocked and both doors swung wide open, your eyes were automatically drawn to the different size test tubes, safety goggles, gas burner, several bottles of some kind of colorful solution, and things you didn't know what they were for. I knew immediately with all this stuff, I could be just like the scientist on the front of the kit! My cousin was overwhelmed because he never saw anything like this before, and all he could say was cool! I advised him he could be my assistant as we started to set up the makeshift laboratory in my bedroom. We were both excited and wanted to fire up the gas burner and boil something in the new glass test tubes.

After getting everything set up, I ignited the burner and adjusted the flame to low as I slowly poured some green stuff I found under the bathroom sink into the test tube, careful not to spill any on the new carpet. I placed the glass test tube in a holder over the low flame and sat back with my cousin to watch the tiny bubbles appear and float to the top. As we watched the liquid boil, we both smiled from ear to ear knowing we were about to create something brand-new. As the glass test tube became hotter, the bubbles got bigger, and I decided it was time to take the test tube off the flame and pour the liquid creation into the glass beaker, only inches away. My cousin was complaining he wanted to do something, so I said he could pour our new creation into the beaker. As he picked up the glass test tube, he accidently dropped the green concoction all over the new carpet. The spill was so hot; the carpet started to steam as we both ran out of the room to get paper towels.

As we soaked up the scientific spill area, we noticed the odor and realized the carpet had changed colors, and some of the fibers were shriveled up. I think my cousin nearly passed out, and his face turned a deep shade of red. I had to think fast since my mom could come downstairs to the washer and dryer at any time. She already told both of us not to rough house in the basement and to make sure we both took our shoes off so we didn't get the new carpet dirty! I told my cousin as I packed up the laboratory as fast as I could, to travel to the bathroom and flush the steaming green experiment down the toilet. He then helped me rearrange my bed and nightstand to cover the scientific spill.

Minutes later, my mom appeared out of nowhere as if to catch us doing something wrong and asked what we were up to. I explained my cousin and I were rearranging some of my furniture, and when we were finished, we were going outside to play. She said okay and started her laundry, and my cousin and I ran upstairs to get out of the house. My cousin said he was sorry and owed me one for not telling on him and getting him in trouble. I said okay, and we ate lunch at his house. Even though I didn't like my bed in the new location, I put up with it, and I was right back were I started in the old basement because now there was a faint odor of something strange from the spill, and it stayed around for a long time.

25

Boy Scout Memories

When I was in grade school, I joined the Boy Scouts and was so excited to wear the uniform, go camping, earn merit badges, sleep in a sleeping bag, and eat food from a real camp fire. My number one memory of camping was one time in the middle of winter, our troop had the privilege to camp out in a cabin with wood bunk beds and a huge fire place. The cabin had an old wood plank floor, real wood paneling on the walls, and only a few windows. When I think about it, I can still see and smell the inside of that cabin. The cabin had no indoor plumbing or kitchen, but there was electricity, and the fireplace was so large you could literally bend over and walk inside!

When that anticipated Friday afternoon finally came, we all met at school and packed our gear in the bus and started the drive to the Boy Scout ranch. We arrived at the cabin just before dinner and unloaded the bus as the sun set slowly, and it began to snow and get colder. We were paired off in fours and instructed to search for firewood before the snow covered the ground. The cabin was in the middle of a forest with a winding dirt road that led from the main highway to the Boy Scout cabin. Since the forest was thick, we all found wood and kindling quickly and headed back to the cabin to get out of the cold weather.

As everyone made it back and was accounted for, the scoutmaster started the fire, which warmed the cabin up in no time. We all started to lay out our sleeping bags on the bunk beds as the roaring fire snapped and popped, and I chose the top bunk for my sleeping quarters, and I even got a window. As the cabin warmed up and the scoutmaster started our supper, everyone was excited about the first night in the cabin. As I looked out the window, I noticed we gathered the firewood just in time because the snowflakes were coming down strong, and they were huge flakes. About forty-five minutes later, we got the call to come over to the giant wood picnic tables because we were almost ready to eat. We brought our own drinks we packed in our backpacks, and we were all hungry and tired. We said a prayer before we ate and then the scoutmaster brought over baked potatoes wrapped in aluminum foil, bisquick rolls, baked beans, hamburgers, and everything tasted out of this world. We ate to our hearts' desire, and there were still some leftovers. Our bonus was everyone sitting on the floor in front of the giant fireplace, eating ice cold watermelon. All this great food and us cozy by the fireplace coupled with the snowstorm outside made me feel safe and sound, and it doesn't get any better than that. As we finished our desert and felt the warmth of the roaring fire, we made a last call to the outside restroom and got ready to retire to our assigned bunk beds. As I climbed into the upper bunk bed, exhausted from a long day, I zipped up my sleeping bag, and with one eye still open, gazing at the roaring fire, I fell into a deep sleep almost immediately.

During the night, I was awakened by the snapping and popping of the logs in the fireplace, as I observed our scoutmaster with a cigarette barley clinging to his lower lip, attending to the fire. I felt a secure feeling that everything was okay and fell back to sleep. The next morning was unbelievable. We got up and dressed and headed outdoors to shovel a path from the cabin to the outside restroom. The cold crisp air and huge snowflakes had continued to fall all night long and had gently layered two feet of snow everywhere.

As a young boy, two feet of snow looked like ten feet, and we had a blast shoveling the paths and throwing snowballs. As we were working outside, the scoutmaster was busy once again preparing tasty tidbits for breakfast. Once the snow had been shoveled, more firewood brought in and everyone thawed out, it was time for breakfast. He had prepared potatoes, eggs, ice cold orange juice, and bread, and we were filled to the brim. Our second day consisted of hiking, tracking, merit badge work, and animal watching, which took most of the day. While on the trail, we had our backpacks with the cold drinks we brought from home, and we were all introduced to spam with crackers and were told that when you're hungry, just about anything taste good on the trail. We got back late that night but had a great time.

The weekend went super fast, and we all had fun and were telling stories around the fire drinking hot chocolate we made from melting our own snow. We all fell asleep quickly that night from another exhausting day. Morning arrived as we started to pack our gear and eat our last breakfast at the Boy Scout ranch. The same nonstop roaring fire that kept us warm and cooked all our meals was sadly, now being extinguished and the cabin cleaned for the next Boy Scout troop.

The memories of that weekend, even as an adult, still echo in my mind whenever I day dream about camping in the winter as a Boy Scout. As I grew older and advanced to the eighth grade, our Boy Scout troop traveled to the mountains for a two-week jamboree. We were told ahead of time that the mountains have bears and deer and other wildlife, and this outing would be very educational. I was so excited I packed for weeks before the final day, making sure I had my brownie camera, sleeping bag, beef jerky, pistachio nuts, and enough clothes for my two-week trip. We traveled by train and got to see real buffalo and eat in the glass top railcars, and I even found out that when you flushed the toilet and looked straight down, you could see the tracks go by. Just to make sure of what I was seeing, I stuffed a roll of toilet paper in the toilet, flushed it, ran to the back of the railroad car, and saw it bouncing and unrolling as the train started up a hill.

When we arrived at the Boy Scout ranch, we were divided up by our troop numbers and introduced to our scout leader for the next two weeks. We set up camp for the first night and got plenty of sleep for the next day's hike. The next morning came quickly as we all rolled out of our sleeping bags, fell into formation, and hiked to the mess hall for breakfast. After packing up all our gear, we headed for the mountains and started hiking through the woods watching for wildlife and paying attention to the signs advising which route was ours to follow. On this hike, we ate a familiar food known as spam. Back in those days after opening the can, you had to rinse off all the slime with your canteen water and then cut it up and eat it with crackers. When you're hiking and hungry, anything tastes good.

Later that afternoon, we arrived at our campsite, and our scoutmaster advised us to secure all our sweet items in a tee shirt and hoist it up a tree to keep the bears from entering our tents. Later that night when the fire burned down and everyone was fast asleep, I went to roll over and found out I had rolled outside the tent and had been sleeping right under the rope holding up our sweets in the tree. It scared me to death, and I crawled back to the tent and secured the flap. The next morning, we hiked up a hill to a makeshift kitchen in the woods and ate breakfast. Just as we were ready to leave and hike back to our campsite, the skies opened up and poured rain for about thirty minutes. It rained so hard you couldn't see five feet in front of you. When the rain stopped, we hiked back to camp only to find out a small river ran right through our tent and washed away our gear nearly seventy-five feet away. We packed up all the wet gear and got back on the trail. Everything went smooth for the next week, and we had a lot of fun finding deer and watching the wildlife until one morning our scout leader never got up. We hiked to his tent and found out quickly he was very sick. I took it on myself to get two friends and advised everyone else to stay with our sick scout leader, and we would hike down the mountain and get help. My friends and I started the hike, and within four hours, we were on the other side of the mountain and arrived at a ranger shack. We advised the ranger what had happened, and he immediately called for a helicopter to fly to the top of the mountain. The rangers carried the scout leader by stretcher to the helicopter landing zone, loaded him inside, secured the stretcher, and then flew him to a hospital. One of the rangers stayed back and guided the remainder of the scouts back down the mountain, and we all joined up for supper. That was my last outing with the Boy Scouts, and the following year, I started high school.

26

Early Age Technology

My grandfather had past away, and years later, my grandmother remarried and moved out of our duplex. I do remember however, right after she got married, she and her new husband stayed in the house a short time while they were looking for a new home.

One day, my brother and I went over to their side of the basement from a connecting basement door my mom told us never to open. As we traveled around the basement, we saw things covered up with sheets that looked like ghosts, but we couldn't turn on a light for fear my grandma and new grandpa might find us. We traveled by touch over to a window and found a small wooden door painted the same color as the walls. As we opened the squeaky faded door, the basement lights suddenly came on, and my brother and I thought we were caught red-handed. We quickly jumped inside the secret passageway and with our hearts beating a mile a minute, we stood there and listened to the footsteps coming down the stairs. My brother and I never said a word, but we could hear something going on, which sounded like a newspaper rattling around. We could hear the newspaper noise, and then it would stop.

Then the paper noise would start again, and then it would stop. Finally, when the noise stopped, I cracked opened the secret door to see what it was. As the door was opening slowly, I could only think that this could be an intruder. Were my grandma and grandpa getting robbed and the bandits wrapping up their silverware in newspaper? What could it be? As I looked around the opened door, I started to laugh and closed it as fast as I could. My brother asked why I was laughing, and I told him to take a look. As my brother opened the door, he also closed it quickly and started to laugh. We both saw our new grandpa sitting on the toilet with his pants down to his knees, doing his duty reading the paper. The reason he didn't see the door opening and closing as we took a peak at him was because of the newspaper. We were laughing as hard as we could but trying to keep quiet, and it's a wonder he never heard us. It was some time before we heard the toilet flush and those footsteps traveling back up the stairs, and then finally the door closing to the basement.

As soon as we heard the door close, my brother and I hightailed back to our side of the basement but never told my mom or dad what we saw. When my grandma and grandpa found a house and moved out, my parents decided to remodel the whole house. It seemed like forever, but eventually, the huge undertaking was completed; and the new floor plan consisted of seven bedrooms, four bathrooms, a full basement and attic, a four-car garage, and a swimming pool. This was a huge improvement, and we had plenty of space to play even on unpleasant days.

One day I came up with the idea to install a speaker in the pool area so my whole family could enjoy music while swimming. My dad had a consol record player in the living room, but that particular room was on the other side of the house. I thought about it for a day or two and came up with an idea. Later that week, I was "home alone" and put my plan into action. My dad was not a mechanically inclined person, so we never had many tools around the house. I gathered up what I could find, which consisted of an old rusted hammer, a large screwdriver, a pair of pliers, and a box of wire I found left behind from the remodeling job.

I began the first phase of my plan by using the pliers to pull back the carpet in the living room where the consol sat innocently in the corner. I eventually, with the help of the screwdriver, was able to pull back the corner of the carpet and began to pound away with the rusty hammer and oversized screwdriver, slowly chipping a hole through the floor into the basement. It seemed like hours chipping away at the plywood until at last, I broke through. The hole turned out to be quite large as I lowered the screwdriver tied to a string into the basement. I ran downstairs to find the location, searching one room after another. I searched for a few minutes with no luck, but then, in the distance, I noticed bits and pieces of wood lying on the basement floor. I ran over to the location and was excited as I looked up and saw the end of the screwdriver dangling through the floor, as if the screwdriver was screaming, "Good job, little carpenter!"

I ran up the basement stairs, skipping every other step with excitement, and finished the first phase of my plan by lowering down the wire, which now had to travel to the other side of the house. Once all the wire was pushed through the giant access hole, I tied the balance to the stereo counsel leg and reinstalled the carpet, covering my access hole. Hoping I had enough wire to reach my destination, I began pounding nails into the floor joist and bending them over to hold the wire in place. Inch by inch, I made my way to the other side of the house, slowly running out of nails and wire, and hoped I was getting close to the swimming pool. So far, everything was going according to plan. As I reached the concrete block wall and wiped the gritty dust from my forehead, I realized I had reached my destination. I was smiling ear to ear! I knew the pool was on the other side of this wall!

Now for phase two! I had to somehow get through the concrete block wall. All I could do was continue on with my trusty hammer and oversized screwdriver. As I pounded the handle of the screwdriver as hard as I could, bits and pieces of concrete block rocketed past my head at high speeds as I inhaled tiny white dust flakes floating around my face. I was determined. I had come this far. I had to finish the job before anyone came home. I continued to chip my way through the wall, inch by inch, just as I had seen on TV a hundred times with bad guys doing the same thing trying to escape from jail. I choked on the white-powered dust as time slowly ticked away but finally shining through a small crack in the concrete wall; I could see the presence of daylight gleaming into my eyes. What a sight! I finally made it to the outside of the house.

I began to pick up the pace and work even harder and faster, knowing I was only inches away from the outside world. It seemed like only minutes later when the breakthrough finally happened. A large piece of concrete block fell off the wall and bounced toward the swimming pool. I had made it; my job here was almost complete. I put down my tools, pushed the last of the wire through the hole, and ran outside to see where I broke through. To my amazement, the hole on the outside of the house was about ten times the size of the hole on the inside. I could almost fit my head inside the concrete block! I knew that was bad and had to think fast; time was ticking away.

I quickly ran out to the garage to see what I could find and to my amazement, found an old caulk tube with a nail stuck in the tip. I figured it was leftover from the remodel job and quickly loaded it into an old rusty caulk gun and ran back to the access hole in the concrete block. After pulling the balance of the wire through the wall, I squeezed the last of the caulk all around the edges of the large piece of block and carefully fitted it back into position, as if finding the last piece of a jigsaw puzzle. I pushed with all my might to make sure the concrete boulder was firmly in place and then started my clean up. I set a pool chair in front of the wiring and set a small table on the other side. I had to get everything back in place even though I wasn't finished. My mom and dad would be home soon, and I didn't want to show them my surprise until I had everything completed.

That night, I slept like a log from all the hard work; but in the morning, I was refreshed and ready to complete my mission. It was Saturday, and breakfast was over, and my mom and dad left to run an errand. I knew I only had a short time to finish the job, so I went back to work and began to wire an old speaker from a radio in the pool area. After completing the speaker and setting it on the table, I ran into the house to figure out how to wire the other end to our stereo. After a half hour or so, I finally figured out the hook up, and music was playing not only in the house but in the pool area as well. I quickly put everything away and got ready to reveal the big surprise to my mom and dad! Finally, after what seemed hours and hours, they pulled in the driveway and brought in some groceries. I was so excited I met them at the door! The first thing my mom said is, "Why is the stereo on and did you clean up your bedroom?"

I replied I had something to show them! As we walked to the other side of the house, I could hear the music getting louder and louder. I opened the door to the pool area and ran outside with a big smile on my face. "Look, Mom and Dad, I wired up a speaker so we can listen to music while we're swimming."

My mom said, "That's nice, but go find your brother and get started cutting the grass."

My heart sank as I walked outside, but I was already thinking of my next project!

27

Weeds and Gas and Fire, Oh My!

As I yawned and slowly opened my eyes, I stared at the white ceiling and listened to the rain beating against the window as well as the wind whistling through the trees. I had big plans for the first day of my summer vacation, but it sounded like I would be trapped indoors for the day. It seemed like the rain was coming down harder as I crawled out of bed and made my way to the kitchen for a bowel of Frosted Flakes, my favorite cereal. I liked Frosted flakes because the cereal tasted good, and when you were finished, you got to drink the sugar-filled milk out of the bowl.

As I looked outside for the very first time, I could see it was pretty nasty. I felt good being safe in the house and wearing my Roy Rogers pajamas. I could barley see the garage through the blistering rain and wind. The trees were bent over from the strong winds as if they were bowing after a stage production, and sticks, leaves, and lawn furniture covered every square inch of the backyard. *So much for playing outside*, I thought as I finished my Frosted Flakes and went into the living room to watch some cartoons. The *Road Runner Show* just started when all of a sudden, the TV went blank. All I could see were lines of black fuzz and a static sound. I quickly flipped through the channels, but everything was the same. I jumped up and ran into the kitchen to tell my mom, but she was on the phone. I listened from the doorway and could hear my dad on the other end. My Mom was telling him she heard on the radio we had a near miss with a tornado touching down in our neighborhood. As I put two and two together, all this weather started to make sense. I ran to take another look outside and could see our TV antenna tower had crumbled from the high winds and came crashing down in the backyard! It was pretty cool to see the giant steal tower, which had always stood a million miles in the air, had crashed in our backyard, right where we always parked our bikes. The twisted, mangled pieces of the antenna were smashed beyond repair! I really didn't care about all the destruction; I just wanted to know when we would be able to watch cartoons again. The next few days were torture without TV and staying in the house instead of being outside riding my bike or building a fort. Luckily, later the next day, we were finally cleared to go outside and play because the rain and wind had finally stopped. What a mess in everyone's yard. Branches, leaves, and lawn furniture from our neighbor's houses were peppered all over our lawn. I had fun walking around the neighborhood looking at all the destruction. Shingles blown off neighbor's homes, windows broken, and small trees pulled out of the ground.

  Later that afternoon, I watched as a big crane installed our new TV antenna. As I stared in the air, the tower was shiny and looked even higher. After the crane left and our TV was working again, we ate supper, watched TV, and had to go to bed.

The next day, I woke up and decided it was a great day to shoot my dad's BB gun. It was an old gun and kind of rusty. The cool thing was the hole in the end of the barrel where the BB comes out, was just the right size to push a stick match inside the barrel. Once you pumped the gun up and pulled the trigger, the BB would launch the match out of the barrel at a hundred miles an hour. If you aimed at a rock or concrete block foundation, the match would start on fire upon impact. I found a large patch of weeds and poured our lawn mower gasoline over the entire site. I dug up a large rock in our neighbor's field and laid it in the middle of the weed patch and loaded my weapon. As I fired the rusted rifle, it seemed like everything was in slow motion. I squeezed the trigger and watched the wood match, with the familiar red tip, launch from the barrel and strike the oversized rock nestled in the middle of the gasoline soaked weeds. Instantly, the entire weed area lit up and danced with fire. I was so proud of my idea as I stood tall and watched the weeds burn out of control. In all the excitement, I forgot to hook up the garden hose, so I ran to the garage and started to unwind the life savor. As I stretched the giant green soaker to the crime scene, I smothered the fire just before it reached our neighbor's wood fence. I was extremely lucky that day because if the wind picked up, I don't think I could have put the fire out.

I learned a huge lesson that day, which was to always have a garden hose ready whenever you're playing with gasoline and matches!

28

Life in the Basement

After my mom and dad had the basement remodeled, my brother and I enjoyed our new bedrooms and bathroom, and we came up with a cool game. When we were playing and my mom yelled down to clean up for supper, we looked at each other with a big smile and got ready for our newly invented game. As we raced to the bathroom, we would each grab a wash cloth and drench it with water. Then we would take turns to see who wanted what end of the basement to hide. With all the lights off and just a small amount of daylight peaking through the basement window, the game would start. If you were lucky enough to hit the other guy with the water logged wash cloth, you got one point. If you launched your towel and missed, the wet towel would stick to the wall, and chances are, you were going to get paid back trying to retrieve your weapon. Whoever had the most points before we were told to get upstairs for supper, was the winner.

My brother and I always enjoyed my mom telling us to get cleaned up for supper. One big item that was in our bathroom downstairs was the furnace. One day, I had filled up my green army squirt gun I received for my birthday and was busy blasting spiders, furniture, and pictures on the wall. My squirt gun had a pretty accurate stream of water because it wasn't the cheap pistol version, it was an army pistol that held a lot of water and had an air pump on the bottom. Once the gun was pumped up to capacity, you could easily hit your target. I had broken my old cap gun a few years back, so I carried my squirt gun in the cap gun holster. I remember it was snowing and a little chilly in the basement that day, and I was glad to be indoors having water fun. After filling up my weapon for the third time, I was pulling fast draws and shooting everything in site. I thought I saw a monster sneak into the bathroom, so I pulled my weapon from my silver-studded holster and slowly made my way into the room. *I can shoot this monster without turning the lights on*, I thought as I walked slowly into the dark unknown. Once in the pitch black room, I could see a shadow dancing on the wall, moving in different sizes. I didn't know what I was looking at, nor have I ever seen anything like it. Luckily, I had my weapon drawn and pumped up and was ready to fire at any moment. As I took one short step after the other, I held my breath and got closer and suddenly saw teeth and something inside dancing and flickering, which looked like the monster reflection I saw on the wall.

As I studied the situation, I found out it was just a tiny flame someone forgot to put out. There was no monster in the room, and the teeth were just the front grill of the furnace, and the little flame must have leaked out somehow. I decided to play quick draw and shoot the flame out and then proudly advise my mom and dad I saved our house from starting on fire. It took a few shots because of the grill, but I finally put the flame out. As I walked back out of the room, I took careful aim and emptied my gun on the rest of the basement walls.

The next morning, I was playing on the basement floor, and I could hear my mom and dad talking and as they were on their way down the steps. They told me there was no heat in the house, and my dad looked around the furnace but didn't know what was wrong. They went back upstairs to place a phone call, and I went back to playing with my army men. Later that morning, a repairman showed up, and I watched him as he took the furnace grill off to look inside. It was at that moment I remembered I forgot to tell my mom and dad about saving us from the house fire. I watched as the repairman reached inside the furnace and turned a knob, lit the flame, and the furnace started right back up. He spent another twenty minutes checking everything he could, trying to find out how the flame could blow out. My mom and dad came down as the repairman was putting the furnace back together, and I heard him explaining he didn't know how the flame went out, and it's very unusual it happened. I continued to play on the floor and acted like I didn't know what they were talking about and decided I wouldn't tell my mom and dad about saving the family from a house fire. I knew that the house now had heat, but if I were to tell them I shot out the flame, I too would be receiving some heat, from a ruler.

As the house warmed up, my mom told my brother and me to practice the piano, which was our five-day-a-week routine. My brother always went first and then went up stairs to watch TV and then it was my turn; and on Sunday, my dad would listen to both of our lessons. The thing I hated about Sunday was the room always filled up with smoke since my dad was a chain smoker. He smoked camel cigarettes with no filter and would take his last puff from the old cigarette to light the new one. When my brother went first for his lesson, my dad was just getting warmed up; and by the time it was my turn, I had a hard time finding the piano, and his ashtray was filled to the top.

One night as I was starting my hour practice, I had an idea. I would practice as usual, but this time I would record the lesson with my tape recorder. The following day after my homework, I quietly climbed to the top of the basement stairs with my trusty tape recorder, set the volume so my mom would be able to hear through the basement door, and then played with my army men until my lesson was finished. I never told my brother, but I always had a blast playing different games as my recorder did all the work. My dad never caught on; he just thought my brother was a superior piano player because I never knew my lesson.

29

007

My brother and I bought an intercom system at our local hobby store, and after a year or so, it ended up collecting dust on a shelf. Years later, I was in the basement looking for something and found the intercom and thought of an idea. The system had a master speaker, which contained a volume knob and on off switches, but the second speaker had no controls. I wanted to wire it up to my cousin's bedroom next door, and when I told them about this great idea and how we could talk back and forth and our moms and dads wouldn't know, they were all for it.

The next challenge was how to get the intercom wire from my bedroom to their bedroom next door, and their bedroom was on the second floor. I watched the phone company on our street many times pull a wire from the telephone pole to someone's house, and my intercom wire looked the same, so I figured I could do it too. I tied one end of the wire to my closet door knob, pushed the balance of the wire out the window, and ran outside to look at our massive antenna tower and could barely see the top. I already knew I couldn't run the wire underground, so I tied the wire around my waist, stuffed my string and knife in my back pocket, and started to climb the tower. As I climbed higher and higher with both hands secured at all times on the cold hard steel, I still was scared, and I didn't want to look down. It seemed the wind was getting stronger the higher I climbed. The tower was moving from side to side, but I knew it had to be safe because I saw the TV guy climb to the top to hook up the new antenna. As I climbed higher and higher, I finally got to the point where I could see into my cousin's bedroom window. It seemed like an hour had gone by as the tower weaved from one side to the other. I now hung on with one hand and wrapped my leg through the rungs of the tower and tied off the wire with my other hand. At one point, I needed both hands to tie the knot and had to leave go of the tower to finish the process. As I glanced down just for a second, everything seemed so small that you could fit it in a doll house. I was nervous and happy and at the same time, realizing the scary part was over as I proceeded slowly down to earth. I walked next door with the balance of the wire and threw it up to my cousin who was watching me the whole time and already had his window open. We screwed the speaker to the wall, pulled the excess wire tight, and hooked up the device. I told him I would call on the intercom when everything was hooked up in my bedroom. Minutes later, I called on our 007 device, which was a total success, and the voices were crystal clear. My brother and I enjoyed hours of fun with the intercom system, and little did my cousins know, we could turn it on at any time and listen to what they were talking about.

  Days later, my mom and dad were gone, so I called my cousins and told them to watch me on our roof. They were huddled at the window as I hiked up our TV antenna tower and headed over to the edge of the house. Our garage was not connected to our house, but I wanted to see if I could jump from our house roof to the garage roof, which looked close enough. I walked to the peak of our house, turned around, waived to my cousins, and ran down the roof picking up speed and at the last minute, jumped with all my might and landed on the garage roof. I could hear cheering from my cousins and talk about a thrill—this was the best. Now all I had to do is get back on the house roof. I backed up to the peak of the garage, started to run to pick up speed, and jumped landing safely on the house roof. As I was bragging to my cousins what a great 007 agent I was, I continued walking with a stride to the other end of the house. As I peered over the roof at the pool, it seemed close enough that if I got to the top of the house and ran fast, I could pick up enough speed, jump out far enough to miss all the concrete deck, and land safely in the deep end of the pool. I was amazed at myself coming up with these great ideas. I told my audience I would be right back and to stay put for the next 007 event as I climbed down the antenna tower to get my bathing suit. I was ready and on the roof in no time as the cheers from the audience began. As I traveled to the peek of the roof and began to run as fast as I could, I realized it was more difficult to pick up speed without shoes on. I got to the edge of the roof, gave it all I had and jumped, and just barely made it into the pool. I missed the concrete deck by about two inches, which was too close for comfort. About three minutes after splash down, I heard my mom yell out the door, asking why I was in the pool with no one home. I told her I dropped one of my toys in the water, and I was getting it out. I was scared and learned my lesson that afternoon and never tried that jump again.

30

I Never Inhaled

I mentioned in one of the stories that my dad was a chain smoker, and our kitchen cabinets really didn't need any handles on the doors. All you had to do is press your hand flat, pull back, and the door would open. The doors were very sticky and disgusting. As a child growing up in this kind of atmosphere, you don't know any better. I remember my dad lighting up cigarettes one after another, seven days a week.

One day I was in my parent's bedroom and noticed a pack of Camel cigarettes on my dad's dresser. I pulled out the bottom drawer to step on so I could reach the cigarettes, and after getting the pack down and pulling one out of the pack, I put it in my mouth just like my dad did and fired it up his shinny Zippo lighter. As the flame got closer to the cigarette, nothing happened. The end of the cigarette turned black but wouldn't light. I threw that one in the trash can and helped myself to the second one. This time I figured out what was wrong and turned the cigarette around so the word Camel was closest to my mouth. I fired up the chrome Zippo once again, and nothing happened. The end of the cigarette turned black again and would not ignite. I was convinced at this point that the pack of cigarettes was no good, and that's why my dad left them on his dresser.

Suddenly, I got a great idea. Why not make my own cigarette?

I ran to the bathroom and grabbed an empty toilet paper roll out of the waste paper can and lightly stuffed it with toilet paper. I ignited his Zippo lighter again and lit my cigarette, and as I lifted the home made concoction to my mouth, I started to cough and accidently sucked in a large flame. I burned my throat and quickly threw the contraption in the toilet. After cooling my mouth down with cold water from the sink, I looked at my throat in the mirror and was amazed at my red scorched throat. I knew for sure after I cleaned the mess up, I would treat myself to some ice cream. I didn't want to reach in the toilet to get the burned evidence, so I flushed the cardboard roller and toilet paper and somehow, it made it down the drain. From now on, I figured I'd let the smoking up to my dad because it was too dangerous and confusing to me.

31

It Wasn't Me!

When I was out at night playing on our dead-end street, it was usually pitch black in spots because we lived in the country and didn't have many street lights. Once in a while, you could tell our neighbors were going to have company because their porch light would be on and covered with three thousand bugs. One time I accidently broke a vase on a ladies porch, and she came storming out to see what all the commotion was. As I was running away, I didn't want her to know who I was, so I ran to a neighbor's house to make her think I was one of their kids. After catching my breath and waiting a short time, I slowly looked around the corner of the house to see if she went back indoors. I didn't see her, so I ran home. I thought this was a cool idea, running to a neighbor's house in case I ever needed an escape route again.

One day, my sister happened to be in the garage as I ran home from another accident, and she said she saw everything and was going to tell Mom. I quickly explained I was glad to see her, and I had a cool trick to show her. Being young, she agreed and for a split second forgot about telling on me. I grabbed some thick string hanging on a rusty nail in the garage that my mom used to tie back her rose bushes when they got too tall. I explained to my sister I was going to show her an escape trick, and I needed her to cross one hand on top of the other. As she put her wrists together, I raced to secure her hands with the thick string. Once the string had several knots in it, I tied the remaining string to the overhead garage door handle. Knowing the knots were good and tight, I walked over to the side door where the button was for the automatic garage door; and as I pushed the button to raise the overhead door, my sister's arms began to rise with the door. When the overhead door was above her head and her weight shut the mechanism down, her arms were stretched high and tight, and she started crying. I told her if she ever told Mom what she saw that night or said anything about me tying her up, I would catch her when she least expects it and do it again. She was scared to death and promised me she wouldn't tell, so I used the lawn trimmers and cut her loose. My secret for certain accidents in the black of night was safe for now, and my mom or the neighbors never did find out.

32

Fireworks to Rockets

One of my favorite pastimes is fireworks. As a young person, I always found someone who would sell them to me. I think my first adventure were cracker balls. They looked like jawbreakers, very colorful, and if you threw them down on a driveway or sidewalk, they would explode, leaving a signature black burn mark. You could also lay them across busy streets and watch cars slow down after they ran over them thinking they might have a blown a tire. From there, I advanced to firecrackers. I used these for blowing up army men, or exploding small tin cans filled with gasoline. From there, I moved on to all sorts of aerial explosions, which would light up a summer evening sky. Everything from bottle rockets fired out of our house chimney to large missals mounted on a stick. I think it was during this time of experimentation that I started to investigate model rockets and solid fuel engines. I started with a solid fuel engine super glued on top of my model cars. I would light the fuse and watch them travel down the driveway at a high speeds, almost tearing the wheels off and then exploding and catching on fire.

My first rocket kit I ever bought took me a long time to put together because I knew it would fly to the moon and back, and I wanted it to be strong and reusable. I had so much fun, lighting the fuse, running away, and turning back just in time to see the sparks from the solid fuel engine igniting, the sound of the roaring engine and the black trail of smoke as the rocket lifted high into the sky. I must have launched that rocket a million times because it was looking pretty ragged as time went on. I decided one day to fill a small plastic cylinder with gasoline, which fit inside the pay load in place of the parachute. This was going to be the final launch. I lit the fuse and stood back as the Silver Arrow launched high into the sky. The sound of the engine and the trail of the black smoke was just a warning that in a few seconds, the rocket would be gone forever. Just then, a huge burst of fire and a loud explosion could be seen and heard around the world. It was the coolest thing I ever saw. As the rocket was speeding back to earth with no parachute to slow it's entry into the atmosphere, flames could be seen from a far as the limp rocket crashed and burned, ending its last flight forever!

Later on, I was in a basement of a commercial building and found some cardboard tubes. They were a little bit larger in circumference and twice the length of Christmas wrapping paper tubes and much, much thicker. I knew immediately this could be my next home made rocket. Time had passed since the Silver Arrow had blown up in flight and lit the sky up for miles, so I was pumped with excitement thinking about a new rocket.

I remember it was a Saturday when I started to collect all the parts and stock piled them in the basement for my new project, which I named the Silver Arrow Two. I found some powdered concrete patch in the garage left over from our remodel job in the basement, commercial glue of some kind, and a plastic tube, which resembled a drinking straw, only longer. As I started construction on the new rocket, I spread the commercial glue carefully on one end of the tube and then the other. I secured both tubes together on a workbench, which meant the new rocket was over six feet long. While the tubes were drying, I started to sand down a block of balsa wood to resemble a nose cone and tail fins, and when completed, I would give them two or three coats of paint. Sanding the nose cone and tail fins took me into the night, but I completed the tiring task and called it a day.

The night went by fast, and after inhaling my breakfast the next morning, I ran down to the work area and examined everything from head to toe. The nose cone and tail fins looked great, and the tubes glued together very well. The painted tail fins and nose cone were painted a gloss black, and you could see your teeth in the shine. I knew the glued tubes were not strong enough and could break apart during flight due to extreme pressure, so I mixed up the concrete patch powder and, with a paint brush, I saturated the tubes. This time I would only have to wait a few hours for everything to dry according to the directions on the can. One of the parts I found laying around in the garage was a large plastic tube, which resembled a drinking straw, only it was about four feet tall. It was made of very hard plastic and would work just fine for a "launching guide" to keep the rocket headed straight as the solid fuel engine propelled it into space. Several days had passed as I checked off in my mind the final stages for the the Silver Arrow Two completion. I had already built the launching pad made of wood covered with a soup can I cut up and nailed down so nothing would catch on fire during the launch. The hard plastic drinking straw was glued to the side of the rocket and would slide over a hanger I took apart and secured in the middle of the launching pad, which would help guide the rocket straight during ignition.

While everything was drying, I rode my bike to the hobby shop and purchased my first ever high tech solid fuel engine, and it was the most money I ever spent for a rocket engine. I bought the biggest they had on the shelf and would have to customize the engine holder to make it fit the rocket. The Silver Arrow Two was two and a half times larger than the original Silver Arrow. While the customized parts I engineered for the engine, consisting of pieces from my erector set and glue were drying, I preceded to construct the last important part that would save the rocket's reentry into the atmosphere, and that was the parachute. I looked and looked all over the house to see what I could use. Our towels were too heavy. I couldn't use our sheets because my mom would see the pieces cut out.

Then it came to me! In my magic set, I had all kinds of silks in all different colors. I raced to my bedroom and dug out what I needed from my magic box and ran back to the basement and started to work. I didn't know how to sew and decided to use my brothers' stapler to connect the silks. Once the parachute was complete, my checklist for the Silver Arrow Two was also complete and ready for launch! The next morning was a big let down because it was too windy, so I had to call off the launch but rescheduled for the next morning at sunrise. I couldn't sleep well that night tossing and turning worrying if I had forgotten anything or if the chute would open on time and stay together with just staples or if my hand-made balsawood parts with the shinny gloss black paint would survive outer space. Somehow I fell asleep, and morning came quickly.

After finishing a big bowl of Frosted Flakes, I started to prepare for the launch, carefully carrying each piece to the launch site. Several neighborhood kids, some bringing there own lawn chairs, started to form a small crowd at the launch site waiting area, ready to get a firsthand look at this enormous rocket. Nobody had ever been this close to a homemade rocket, especially over six feet tall. It took me about a half an hour to set the launch site up, and now it was time. As I started the countdown out loud from ten and then nine, suddenly all the kids joined in, eight, seven, six, five, four, then I lit the fuse, three, two, one; and a second later, the engine ignited! Everyone heard the beautiful deep sound of the engine thrust and enjoyed the dark trail of smoke as the rocket shot straight up in the air at a million miles an hour. Everyone watched as it traveled higher and higher and higher. It looked like a dot in the sky it was so high, almost above the clouds. Then I saw the engine exhaust blow out and the parachute opening in slow motion. It was beautiful! The homemade six-foot Silver Arrow Two had accomplished what it was built for and now was descending back into the atmosphere with the help of handmade parachutes made from my magic kit. The rocket seemed to be hanging in midair so everyone in the world could enjoy it. All the kids were cheering and clapping! It couldn't have been a better launch. Suddenly, as I was watching the rocket descending back to earth in slow motion, reality hit. The rocket wasn't coming home. The winds were very strong at that height and started to carry the rocket in the opposite direction from the launch site. I didn't really prepare for recovery of the rocket; I assumed it would come straight down. The high tech engine propelled the Silver Arrow Two much higher than I expected. You could have heard a pin drop as everyone watched helplessly as the rocket drifted over the river and turnpike and then into the next neighborhood. All of us just stood there, which seemed like a lifetime, until the silence was broken by one of the neighbor kids, yelling, "That was the coolest thing I ever saw."

    I became a legend in my neighborhood that day because everyone thought the launch was planned this way, and the rocket was never supposed to come back. I left the story that way because I liked being a legend and because some of the children who still live on the street are now adults and still talk about that story. For several days after the launch, I hunted for the Silver Arrow Two on my bike, not telling anyone, but never found it. I'll never forget that rocket or the fun I had making it!

33

Big Red Tomatoes

Before my brother and I ever worked for my dad's business, he thought it would be a good idea to send us out into the world for some training—that is, to pick tomatoes for a summer. My brother was fifteen years old, and I was twelve. We were young, and I guess we trusted my dad to make sure we both were going to have fun at this tomato job. My brother and I never saw a tomato field or even knew how tomatoes grew! I remember we got up early one hot morning in June, ate breakfast with my dad, and when we finished, we crawled into the station wagon and headed downtown. We had no idea where we were going; in fact everything looked strange and unfamiliar to us. My dad pulled the car over at some building in the middle of town and told us he would see us tonight and to go inside and give the man our names. I remember I was scared to death because of all the people standing around and looking at us, and I couldn't understand what they were saying. I found out later on as I got older that this office my dad dropped us off at was some kind of a job placement firm that finds the unemployed jobs, and business owners can call in to hire laborers for the day. The majority of the people there were of another culture that we never experienced before, which is why we couldn't understand them.

That morning, my brother and I learned that there are a lot of different kinds of people in the world. Some of them looked scary, had beards and holes in their clothes and no teeth. I was thinking I can't wait to get out of this place and get to the tomato job so we could be safe and relax a little bit. My brother went up to the counter and left me with all the people staring at me, and he told the man at the counter our names. The man gave my brother some paperwork and then he came back to wait with me. It seemed like an hour had gone by and then the man at the counter called our names and told us to go outside for our ride. I thought maybe my dad was back, and we were going with him; but to my surprise, we saw a huge farm truck with a ladder down the bumper, and we were told to get aboard. I thought this would be cool because we never got to ride in the back of a big truck with no top on it. My brother and I were the first ones on, and I thought maybe we would be the only two.

As we waited and watched, I think every person in that lobby was now on the truck, and we were getting squeezed to death because there was no more room. The ride was dusty, bumpy, and long, and we couldn't understand what the people were talking about. After traveling down a dirt road out in the middle of nowhere and swallowing a gallon of dust, the truck came to a stop, and everyone started to get off.

Suddenly, a man appeared out of nowhere and told us we get paid nineteen cents per hamper and to start picking as soon as we got off the truck. My brother and I already knew what a hamper was because we had one at home that we put our dirty clothes in. Within minutes, we found out that a tomato hamper is a V-shaped basket. I never worked so hard in my life. I had to drag the hamper with me, bend over and pick the tomatoes, fill the hamper to the top, and then carry it back to the truck. The man who loaded them on the truck took your name and marked down how many you brought him. Then I grabbed another empty hamper and walked back out to the field to start all over again. As I was about halfway back, I could see a truck driving slowly, and two men in the back were throwing something out into the fields. All the workers were running toward whatever they were throwing out, and as I got closer, I could see it was plastic gallon jugs filled with fresh water. My back hurt badly, but the one thing that was worse is my dad never packed our lunch or gave us water to drink. We were too slow and never got any water, so my brother and I went the whole day with no food, no water, and had to listen to people we couldn't understand.

The tomato job for me went on for about two weeks and seemed like a year, and my brother stayed for a total of four weeks. The two weeks for me were the scariest and the hardest I've ever worked. The one thing that sticks out in my mind even to this day is I don't ever remember getting paid. When I asked my brother about it, he just smiled and said I was paid; but since he filled out the original paperwork when we started, I think he collected all the money.

34

Dangerous Maintenance

I think back on some of the dangerous things I've done in my childhood, and one stands out in bold print. I was fifteen years old and working for my dad, and he always had a million things going on. If it wasn't a real estate purchase, it could be a rental problem or something happening at the corporate office.

I remember I was riding home with my dad on a Friday evening, and he was talking about the warehouse sky windows leaking moisture on the cases of beer. He had a roofer check everything on the roof but couldn't find anything wrong. I had no idea what he was talking about or what sky windows were, but I nodded my head anyway, so it looked like I did.

The next day was Saturday, and that meant two things. One, my brother and I could sleep in a little longer; and two, we had to wash trucks and company vehicles. I was in luck because this

Saturday, my brother wasn't around, so I had it easy and just had to wash the company cars. My dad drove me to the office and unlocked everything and told me he had to run some errands but would be back later in the afternoon. I got the hose and all the other wash gear out and started my routine. Before I knew it, I had finished my job; and after putting everything away, I happened to look up, and I saw what my dad was calling sky windows. They had been there forever; I just didn't know their name. It just happened to be a cool morning, and inside the warehouse it was even cooler; so when I looked up, I saw little drops of water coming off the sky windows and dropping on the beer cases, just like my dad told me. I thought about it for a few minutes and thought maybe I could fix the problem. We had some lumber in another warehouse, so I ran over to get it. Some nails and plastic sheets were used for lying on carpet floors when we painted rentals, so I brought all the stuff back but didn't have a measuring tape, so I just looked up and walked off the measurements with my feet and made a mark on the concrete floor with an old rusty beer cap. Once I scraped the floor and had my dimensions, I started to nail the lumber in a rectangular shape. I didn't have anything to cut the wood with, so I made sure the rectangle was at least as big as my scrapes on the concrete and didn't care if it was a little bit bigger.

Next I took our sheets of painting plastic and hammered thumbtacks, threw the plastic and into the wood, stretched the plastic tight, and thumbtacked the other sides so it would look like a window. I used my dad's scissors from his office to cut the excess plastic off, and I thought the finished invention looked great, but now, I had seven more to make. It took me some time to complete all seven because I had to dig through the lumber to get different sizes so they all looked the same, and they all looked nice, and hopefully, I had enough nails. Now that all eight of my "sky window shades" were completed, I forgot to figure out how I was going to hang them and how I would get up that high.

The warehouse ceiling was the equivalent of a two-story building, and we didn't have ladders that would reach that high; and even if we did, there is no way I could put the ladder up by myself. I thought about a couple of things, but then it hit me. We had a large roll of chain in the garage that the drivers would use to hang beer signs in bar windows, and that would work perfectly because the window shades were not heavy. I thought I would use the forklift to pick up a large stack of pallets, raise the pallets up as high as the fork lift would go, and then climb up the side of the pallets like a ladder, and stand on the top pallet to hook up the window shade.

This story scares me to death as I'm writing, but back then, I didn't think twice about crawling to the top of this death trap to hook up the customized window shades I made. The forklift was old, and with the weight of the pallets and the height up as far as it would reach, the forks swayed back and forth as I climbed to the top. I forgot the chain and some tools while I installed the first shade, but once I had everything I needed, I just left it up on top and drove the fork lift to each sky window and hung the shade. After a long day and hard work, I put everything away and was parking the forklift when my dad walked into the warehouse. He asked if I was finished washing everything, and I told him yes and showed him I fixed the leaking problem on the beer cases, and he said, "That's great. Let's go home." And we walked out to the car. I felt like I got the shaft because my dad never looked up or said good job. I think about that now and how I could have fallen off or had one of the pallets break or a number of things gone wrong, I would not be writing this story today! I think I had a whole army of guardian angels working with me that day. Those shades were installed over thirty years ago and are still hanging there today!

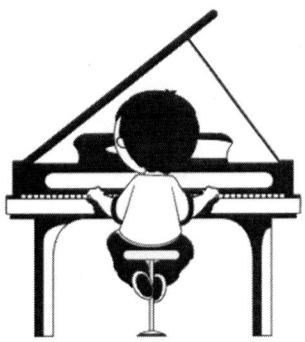

35

The Chello

One day after school, I had an appointment with my uncle who was a dentist. His office was within walking distance from our school, which was past the court house, past the candy store, and then two more blocks. I met up with a friend, and as we started to walk, he asked me if I wanted a coke. I said sure, and he told me to follow him into the court house. I had never been inside before, but the ceilings were miles above my head; and on the main floor, under the stairwell, was an old Coca-Cola machine with tiny bottles of coke, for just ten cents.

My friend deposited two dimes, and we opened the bottles and enjoyed the cold Coca-Cola. As I took my second drink, I heard my name being called and almost didn't swallow everything. As I looked up, I saw my dad walking toward me with a mean look on his face, and he was asking what I was doing in the court house. I told him I was on the way to the dentist and stopped in for a coke, and he blew his top and took the coke and told me to start walking. I left feeling embarrassed in front of my friend and felt bad I didn't get to finish the rest of my coke but headed to my appointment anyway. I arrived on time and immediately, before I could even sit down, the nurse directed me to the dentist chair.

My uncle arrived, dressed in all white, and asked me how I was doing in school. I said okay, and he proceeded to look inside my mouth with a little mirror on a handle. After probing and sticking his fingers throughout my mouth, he said he would have to drill into one of my teeth because he saw a tiny cavity. I must have looked horrified because he told me twice that it wasn't going to hurt. I had my mouth open, eyes closed, and hands gripping the arms of the chair for dear life, as he gave me a shot, which hurt more than the drilling, but after everything was finished I never felt any pain, and the time seemed to go by quickly. My uncle had a big smile on his face and told me he had to get something in the next room. Within seconds, he returned with a Dixie Cup and a small amount of mercury inside. I never played with or touched mercury before, but I knew that's what was in my filling. I thanked him and carried the cup upright as I walked home. I showed my mom what my uncle gave me, and she said that's fine and to get washed up for supper.

This particular night after supper, my brother and I had a piano recital; and my dad would be taking us and told us earlier if we didn't make a mistake, he would by us a milk shake at the ice cream store. We were pretty excited about the milk shakes and staying out past our bedtime because it was a school night, and we never did this before.

After supper, my brother and I got cleaned up and put on our suits, and my dad drove us to the school auditorium. The last thing my Dad said was good luck to both of us, but all I heard was a creamy milk shake and up late on a school night. My brother's class went first, and when he finished, he went out in the audience and sat with my dad. As I stood with my classmates in alphabetical order, it wasn't long, and I was up. I proceeded to go out in front of the audience, and they applauded as I sat down at the piano to play my memorized piece titled "The Chello." I had no problem remembering the notes and played the eighty-eight keys like a professional. I thought everything was going quite well when all of a sudden, I was at the ice cream store ordering my large vanilla milk shake with a bright red cherry on top and a long thick straw stuck in the middle. I raced over to grab a booth by the window so I could see all the cars driving up and down the busy street. All this enjoyment and on a school night yet to boot.

Suddenly, I was thrown back into reality, and I was playing the piano and couldn't remember how to end the song. I thought and thought but couldn't come up with an ending, so I started the song all over again. As I came to the ending the second time, I was still drawing a blank, so I had to end the song by playing, *Ta Da!* The audience applauded as I took my bow and walked off stage, sadden that my dad would yell at me for goofing up, and I would probably have to sit in the car while my brother and my dad drank their milk shakes. I traveled outside to where our station wagon was parked, and my dad and brother were already inside. As I opened the door, ready for the yelling to begin, my brother told me to hurry up because the ice cream store was closing in a half hour. I didn't say anything wanting to make sure I was included in the ice cream, and just then, my dad said he was proud of both of us as we drove out of the parking lot. I had a smile from ear to ear because somehow my dad missed my mistake, which meant I got to stay up late too. That night was one I'll never forget because just like in my dream, we drank milk shakes, sat in a booth to watch the cars drive by, stayed up late on a school night, and the most important thing of all, my dad never caught on that I made a mistake!

The next morning was a Saturday, and I woke up and suddenly remembered that I had the cup with mercury in it and got excited

I had something unique to play with today. After breakfast, I called my cousin to come over to show him my surprise, and we both started to play with the mercury on the tile floor. We pushed it back and forth and tried to smash it and created all kinds of experiments, and later it was time for lunch. As we scooped all the pieces of mercury back into the cup, it formed one ball again, and we both remarked how that was really cool. I walked over to put the cup in a cabinet when my hand slipped, and the mercury spilled out and hit the floor. When it reached the floor, it broke into a million pieces and went in every direction. My cousin and I were on our knees and couldn't find a single piece anywhere. We both laughed about it and went upstairs to eat lunch. About two months later, we had bratwurst for lunch, and I didn't like the taste of that big fat hot dog; so when my mom was on the phone, I snuck downstairs to my bedroom and threw it under a throw rug by my bed and came back up in the nick of time as my mom arrived back in the kitchen, and I told her I cleaned up my plate and wanted to go outside to play. She looked at my plate and told me to put it in the sink and then I could go outside. I had planned to go back to my bedroom to get the big fat hot dog and feed it to my neighbor's dog, but I forgot and went outside. After cleaning up the kitchen, my mom started vacuuming the house. When she reached my bedroom and hit a high spot in the throw rug, she pulled it back and spotted the bratwurst. I was called in from playing, given a spanking for lying and wasting food, and sent to my room. It was at this time while having nothing to do, I was looking under my bed and spotted many tiny balls of dusty mercury laying there and ready to play with again. With the help of a piece of paper, I gathered them up in my hand and went to clean off the dust in the bathroom. As I tried to rinse it off, the whole ball of mercury rolled off my hand and went down the drain. That was the end of playing with mercury, but it was the gift that kept on giving, for awhile anyway!

36

Trash Eliminators

My brother and I started working for my dad's company at a young age. Because of our age, the first job we ever held on the corporate ladder was washing beer trucks, a dump truck, a couple of semi rigs and company cars. Our pay structure started out at twenty five cents an hour. My parents never bought into the "allowance fad" like the rest of the neighborhood kids, so if we didn't work, we didn't get paid. The trucks were huge and time-consuming. We had to wash the entire truck including the top, sweep out the inside with a very small hand brush, empty out the nasty ashtrays, wash the windows inside and out, and wipe the seats down. The job grew old, year after year, so we were glad when my dad moved us up the ladder right after my brother got his driver's license.

Besides the beer company, my dad had rental property, both residential and commercial. Our first new job was to get the dump truck to a rental house on the other side of town and empty all the trash left by the last tenant. As my brother shifted gears and we were talking, it was obvious both of us were excited about moving up the corporate ladder. This would dictate better hours and more money. Now that we were big shots, we passed the "washing opportunity" to our younger cousins. After driving for fifteen or twenty minutes, we knew we were at the right house when we saw all kinds of boxes and rugs on the front porch. My brother backed the truck up to the front porch and unlocked the front door of the house. When we walked in, we knew immediately there was enough work for a few days, and we better get some gloves on. The house had been vacant for a few weeks, and it smelled terrible and was very hot due to the windows being closed. As soon as we pried the painted windows open, we started to haul out the "leftovers" and threw them in the dump truck. The first load took us about a half hour to fill to the top, threw a tarp over the load, and tied it down so nothing would fall out and started our journey to the landfill. I had never been to a landfill, so I was pretty excited to see what this place was all about. When we arrived, the very first thing I noticed was about three million birds and mountain after mountain of trash. The odor in the air could knock your socks off, and so far, I didn't think this place was so cool. My brother pulled the truck on the scale to get us weighed, and the man told us which location to dump the load.

The drive to our location took us about five minutes, and when we arrived, my brother backed up to the pit; and we both watched through the back window as the load dumped and emptied the truck, and we never had to lift a finger. As we were leaving, I spotted something and told my brother to hit the brakes. I jumped out of the truck, and to my surprise, there were a gazillion brand-new flashlights lying on the ground. They were the flashlights that were sealed up with the battery already in it. I picked up about a dozen, and while running back to the truck I was thinking, maybe this place is cool after all.

As we started back to the rental, I opened the package and turned the flashlight on, but nothing happened. Then it dawned on me. That's why they were in the landfill; they don't work. We arrived back at the rental house and took about three more loads to the landfill and then called it a day.

The next day, we were both tired but had to unload the basement of its many treasures, so my brother backed the dump truck to the back door of the house to make it easier on us. My dad told us to get rid of everything in the house, so our next step was to load up an old washer and dryer that weighed about a million pounds. After several attempts to get these heavy monsters up the steps, I came up with a great idea! Let's hook a chain around them and pull them up the steps with the dump truck. My brother smiled and said, "We have the chain. We have the truck. Let's do it!"

We both ran out to the truck to hook a few chains together to make the run from the truck to the basement. Once the washer was chained up and the other end was hooked to the truck, I gave my brother the signal, and he slowly drove away as I watched the washer bang each step until it got to the top landing and then gouged the back door and came to a complete stop at the corner of the porch. We put down the tail gate and pushed the washer off the porch and into the truck and did the same with the dryer. The dryer caught the handrail and tore it off the wall as it was traveling up the stairs, so we would have some repair to do later. We were getting pretty good at this stuff and finished up that load and headed for the landfill. Once again after dumping the load, I spotted another treasure and once again told my brother to hit the brakes. I ran back to the spot, but it turned out to be junk, so I started back for the truck. My brother had crawled to the top of the cab and was watching me and smiling. I found out why he was smiling as I got closer to the truck; he jumped back in the cab and took off. He traveled about an eighth of a mile, crawled back on top of the cab, got comfortable, and watched me walk toward the truck again. I would get close; he would take off. This happened about three or four times, and finally, we were getting close to the front entrance; and he had to let me back in the truck or the guy in the weigh station would see us. Traveling back to the warehouse, we were both laughing and thought this was the greatest job we ever had.

Get ready for more excitement, more new stories, and a touch of danger as you read the chapters to come.

37

Big Band Sounds

My dad played the piano and base and had a thirteen-piece orchestra, which was the house band at a dance hall called Rainbow Gardens. My hometown was between Toledo and Cleveland, Ohio, and my dad opened for some big band names like Benny Goodman, Jimmy Dorsey, and Liberace, just to name a few. These big bands would perform in Toledo and then travel and stay over in our hometown to perform, and then travel to Cleveland to perform and vice versa. It was a huge ordeal back then, and my dad was proud to be part of the history. I remember he would take my brother and me with him during the day to set up, and it was our job to sprinkle wax flakes on the concrete floor, which made the floor slippery for jitter bug dancers. There was also a wishing well made out of stone in the middle of the dance hall, and people would toss coins in hoping their wish came true.

When my dad was finished setting up, and my brother and I were finished with the wax flakes, the dance hall looked pretty good and very inviting. Strings and strings of lights coupled with low wattage old-fashioned light bulbs were hung high in the air and seemed to run back and forth a million times, transforming the dance floor to echo brilliance and class, inviting everyone to have a good time. My brother and I never got a chance to come back when everything was open, and I guess that's because we were underage. One good thing about completing our work is my dad always paid us for helping him by holding our ankles as we got in the wishing well, which was about two feet deep. We would walk on our hands and pick up as many nickels and dimes as we could and then we were allowed to purchase candy at the snack bar. I don't think my brother and I ever missed an opportunity to help my dad set up his band. He wanted to pass on his experience with music to his sons and started both of us out at an early age on the piano. We both took lessons for years, and during that time we played the piano, tenor saxophone, base, and drums. One thing for sure is, my dad never let us listen to rock and roll or country music; he only wanted us to listen to what he approved of. My brother stopped playing when he graduated high school, but I had three more years and had already joined both the marching band and the school orchestra. I settled into the tenor saxophone since I would be marching in the band. Our school was pretty big into music for a small town, and our music class had quite a few members. In the saxophone section alone, we had almost a dozen people.

During the football season, we had to learn to play our new songs, march in straight lines and custom-made patterns because each game was different. As the season went on and the summer temperatures got hotter, so did the band uniform. The marching and sitting on the bleachers during the game was getting boring! The band was always last to get to the snack bar for a cold drink and munchies, and that made me start thinking of a solution. I came up with a great idea that wouldn't help the band so much but would sure solve my problem.

Before leaving the house for the next game, I made sure I packed a few bags of chips, maybe some candy and a can of soda. I packed them in my saxophone carrying case, and when I arrived at the football field, I conveniently converted everything to the inside of my instrument. Just knowing I didn't have to be the last one in line at the snack bar seemed to make the uniforms cooler, the marching less boring, and the night just that much better. During halftime, my soda was still chilled, and the chips and candy hit the spot. Before I knew it, football season was over, and it was time to gear up for the school orchestra. Practicing in the class room meant we didn't have to wear those heavy uniforms; we were inside with air conditioning, real bathrooms, and comfortable chairs. The school orchestra schedule consisted of practice every day after school to get ready for our main event. Practicing song after song for almost an hour, five days a week became a little monotonous and forced me to think out of the box. While sitting in the saxophone section with my friends, I began to add some jazz to the song and put my own spin on what it should sound like. I knew my friends could hear what I was doing because of their laughter as I intervened with harmony and blew away the boredom.

As we got closer to our main event, I was getting better and better jazzing up our songs; and the rest of the saxophone section was on laughter standby, waiting to hear what I would come up with next. Finally, the Saturday night event we were all waiting for arrived. All our practice days were over as we set up the auditorium ready to be packed with proud parents anticipating nothing but good reviews from their children. Everyone looked their best in suits and ties and freshly combed hair as the lights dimmed, and the curtains opened to reveal a surprisingly packed auditorium. Our first song went off without a hitch, and playing in an auditorium rather than a classroom improved the sound five hundred percent! I guess all that practice really did do us some good because it seemed after each song, the applause became louder and louder. I saw my mom and dad dead center in the audience, but I didn't wave or look at them for fear they might call out my name or stand up and embarrass me.

The rest of the night went by fast, and we were about to start our last song for the evening when I thought I would try my "jazz up the song" routine. The orchestra proceeded as I intervened with my jazz and saw smiles leaking out of the corners of mouths from the saxophone section. I thought to myself that this auditorium really makes the jazz sound stand out on its own. I figured it must be the high ceilings and the larger room because this song never sounded like this in the classroom. Then I started wondering if anyone was recording us tonight, and if they were, how big of a tape recorder do you have to manipulate to really capture the whole orchestra? And when you play it back, would it sound the same as it does right know or sound muffled? I didn't remember anyone assigned to record us; or come to think about it, I don't ever remember seeing a recorder. I wonder if I'm the only one thinking about this.

All of a sudden, I was snapped back into reality as the entire orchestra stopped playing because it was the end of the song, and I was daydreaming about a tape recorder. I also came to a complete stop, but it was too late. Two notes leaked out in a high pitch that could be heard around the world. I was so embarrassed but put my horn down at the same time the others did, and no one could tell who did it. Not one smile was cracked as everyone sat stiff in their chairs, and the audience applauded, which seemed like hours.

Finally, the director walked toward the audience and began to speak as the huge colorful drapes closed behind him. Everyone broke into a low-pitched laughter as we all gathered our music and headed out of the auditorium. That night will never be forgotten, and only the saxophone section really knew what happened.

38

Beer Trucks

As my brother and I grew older, so did our responsibilities, and we were putting in more and more hours working for my dad. Besides the occasional rental that needed cleaned out, or a house that needed repair and paint, we moved on to things like unloading and loading all the beer trucks and semis as they arrived, or running a beer route when someone was ill, and my brother working in the office once in a while, side by side with my dad. I noticed as the years went by, my dad's vocabulary seemed to change as he grew older. It seemed like he really didn't care what he said because he could care less what you thought. Thus, a potty mouth was developed, and it seemed like every other word was a swear word. Blank this or blank that, go get blank and put it on the blank truck. This became his normal conversation, and if you did something wrong and he was there, the vocabulary seemed to elevate, and even more words were used that were even brand-new to me.

I'll never forget I was loading a semi-truck one day, and we had two forklifts, one new and one old. I was running the old one with the gasoline engine, and it smoked a lot when you pressed down on the accelerator. There was a fan built through the concrete wall in the warehouse that was supposed to exhaust the fumes outside, but it never did work right. When you were finished loading for the day, your face looked like you were mining coal for a week. I was loading and was almost finished when my dad came out with the paperwork. He always made me nervous standing and staring, and I accidently ran off the loading ramp and dumped a whole pallet of beer, which consisted of forty-nine cases. The forklift bounced back, and I was okay, but there were broken bottles and beer all over the floor. Then all of a sudden out of nowhere, I heard cuss word after cuss word echoing in the warehouse and could see and hear that it was coming from my dad's mouth. It was amazing. I never heard so many cuss words echoing so loud and so quickly in my life. It was like he loaded them up in a machine gun, and now was the time to pull the trigger! After his voice became horse and he walked back to his office shaking his head, my verbal whipping consisted of the following: number one, I will not be driving the forklift for a week; number two, I have to wash out and dry all forty-nine cases whether they needed it or not; and number three, I was not getting a paycheck that week. It took me hours to pick up all the glass, wash, and dry forty-nine beer cases, mop the floor two or three times because the beer was so sticky from the hot warehouse, and then reload all the cases with new bottles of beer. Needles to say, I was very careful after that accident and took my time loading and unloading regardless if my dad was watching or not!

About three weeks after the accident, my dad called my brother and me to his office early one morning. I thought it might be another payroll deduction meeting, but instead he announced my brother had to run a beer route that day because one of the drivers called in sick, and I was tagging along to help out. He also said in the same breath that we were to behave like adults and get back as soon as we could. I know I was trying to hold back any smiles that may jump out of the corner of my mouth at any time due to the excitement of getting away from a smoke-filled warehouse. I think my brother was excited too because this particular day was the day he was supposed to work in the office, side by side with my dad, and inhale cigarette smoke all day. We both said okay and left his office but waited until we got into the warehouse so we could yell with excitement. As we both loaded our beer truck faster than we ever loaded one before, I was daydreaming what a cool day this was going to be. After double-checking our load, I loaded up the handcart and extra gloves and jumped in the passenger side of the truck. We were almost a mile away from the warehouse when it hit us that we would be outside today, and both of us started laughing and pretty happy the driver called in sick.

The route we had was an easy one, and our first stop was the biggest. Since my brother was older and I was underage and not allowed in bars, I would unload the beer and stack it on the handcart, and he would tote them into the bar. I would have the second load stacked up before he could get back outside. We were like a well-oiled machine. He'd bring the empties out, and I would stack them as quick as I could.

By the time lunch came around, we were getting pretty good and fast. We had a huge burger and fries, and I was full. My brother said he would use the bathroom while I finished my soda. I agreed and drank down the last of my root beer and headed for the back door. As I approached the truck, my brother left one of the bay doors open and had started to pull away. He yelled out the window, "If you want a ride home, you better jump in." Just then, he floored the beast and started to pick up speed.

I ran as fast as I could toward the bay door and with all my might at the last minute, jumped and made it safely inside. I could hear my brother laughing out of control as we sped away. I was trapped inside the bay because there was no place to go. I started beating on the cab so my brother would stop and let me ride up front, but he yelled back he couldn't hear me and just kept on driving. I was prisoner in the metal cage for about forty five minutes, and then finally, we arrived back at the warehouse. The truck came to a stop, and I jumped out and could hear my brother still laughing in the cab. We told my dad everything went okay, and as my brother and I headed home, we both agreed that being on the beer route was a lot of fun, and we couldn't wait until the next driver got sick.

39

Quiet on the Set

In the seventh grade, two months before Thanksgiving, my teacher presented the class with an English assignment. I remember the assignment well because she wanted each individual to pick a subject of interest and then compose a story containing a minimum of five hundred words. We had two weeks to complete the project, and our grade would reflect a big portion on our report card. I thought hard about the assignment for almost three days and finally came up with an idea! Instead of writing a five-hundred-word story, I would invite a few of my friends and produce a movie. I knew my dad owned an eight millimeter camera, but back then, cameras had no sound track.

Several years earlier, I received a tape recorder for my birthday, so I knew I had all the tools for a great movie production. I was always intrigued with the show *Mission Impossible* and never missed an episode. I liked the gadgets, excitement, and the missions, which seemed totally impossible to complete before the end of the show yet never stumped or slowed down the *Mission Impossible* team. My movie production would be unique, exciting, and hopefully make the whole class sit at the edge of their chair wondering what would happen next, just like on TV! I copied the title *Mission Impossible* and hoped my teacher had seen the TV show. I had the camera, tape recorder, and crew; now I just needed a plot and a place to film this highly acclaimed and soon-to-be sought-after movie. Three days of my two weeks were already used up trying to think of what to do. A fourth day was burned up getting equipment and the crew rounded up. I had to get into production fast if I were going to make the deadline. Finally, on the evening of the fifth day, I hit the jackpot! I could use my dad's beer distributing warehouse for the filming and use an illegal drug ring for the plot.

The sixth day landed on a Saturday, so early that morning, the crew, sound, and filming technicians, and all the props were ready for action at the beer warehouse. When watching the *Mission Impossible* show on TV, the team always started out with the main actor arriving at a location in an airplane, car, or some type of transportation. He then locates a hidden tape recorder and begins listening to his mission. When the message ended, the tape recorder would start to smoke and then burn up. I would transform myself into the main actor, arriving at the location to listen to the tape recorder to obtain all the valuable information. Since I didn't have a driver's license, I arrived at the beer warehouse on a child's two-wheeled bicycle with training wheels, wearing a sports coat, dress pants, and tie.

I proceeded into the warehouse office to locate my mission, and after searching the office from top to bottom, I found the tape recorder duct taped to the bottom of the service desk. As I pressed "PLAY" on the recorder, the mystery voice welcomed me to the job and explained that the city of Fremont, Ohio was infested with a large drug ring that had been smuggling drugs into the city undetected. My mission, if I were to accept it, would be to infiltrate the drug ring and shut it down forever. If I, or any of my team were caught, our names and whereabouts would be eliminated from the Mission Impossible records. The tape ended by saying, "Good luck, Harold," and then behind the scenes, a smoke bomb was lit and waved in front of the camera to make it look like the tape recorder was smoking and burning up!

Filming that day was long and tedious. Hours and hours were spent setting up props, changing locations, lighting, and reworking scenes that just didn't seem right. Late that Saturday night, the day finally came to an end, and the whole crew went home exhausted! The movie had reached the halfway mark, but I still had many more hours of work adding the background sound track to the entire movie. I think everyone slept like a log that night, and every day for the next week, I came home from school and continued working on the sound track for the movie. I had to record footsteps, voice overs, fight scenes, music, and all the miscellaneous sounds needed.

After long hours and precision background fill in sounds, I finally completed the sound track and very carefully aligned the tape with the starting point of the movie. The first scene of the movie showed me ridding the two-wheeled bicycle up to the front door of the warehouse with the *Mission Impossible* theme song playing in the background recorded from the actual television show.

The homemade movie took hours and hours to produce but only lasted nine and a half minutes. I guess all this hard work filming could compare to a mother preparing the traditional Thanksgiving dinner for the family—preparing, cooking, setting the table, making sure everything is perfect and twenty minutes later, everyone is finished eating. The movie and sound track was completed just in the nick of time, and I transported all the equipment to school and prepared to show the secret weapon to the class.

Our teacher had no idea that my friends and I made this movie, so I stored all the gear at the back of the classroom until it was time. The assignments were to be read out loud in the front of the classroom, and everyone was called alphabetically, so I knew I had a little time and would make sure I introduced everyone associated with the production of the film. I was in a misty haze not hearing much of what others were saying, worrying about what the teacher and my classmates would think, and if the teacher would even let the movie be seen by the class. What would happen if we all failed and received an F on the assignment, and I brought my entire crew down with me?

Then out of nowhere, I thought I heard my name.

Was I dreaming, or did she really call my name? When I came out of the haze and saw everyone looking at me, I knew she really did call me. Still nervous about the production, I mustard up all the courage I had and nervously transported the gear myself to the front of the class. My friends jumped in once everything was up front, and in no time, we had set up all the equipment and were ready to roll the film. With a raspy nervous voice, I explained to the teacher and to the class I had not written the assignment but instead made a movie with a few of my friends for the entire class to enjoy.

All of a sudden, there was an echo of clapping and whistling throughout the classroom, as if everyone mistakenly thought I said there was no school tomorrow. To my surprise, everyone in the room including the teacher was excited to take a break and watch an exciting movie with sound. The lights were turned off, and I started both the tape recorder and the movie projector together without a problem and walked to the back of the room to watch everyone's expressions. I didn't need to watch the movie since I saw it three hundred times before, and as long as the sound was synced with the movie, I didn't need to watch. I saw classmates smiling and laughing, and even the teacher blended in, and it seemed everyone was enjoying the movie. I thought I even heard some wows, and then before I knew it, the movie ended, and the lights came back on. As I was walking to the front of the class, it was a pleasure to be in school that day because of all the applauding and whistling. I called everyone involved with the production to come up front with me because we were all ready to receive our grade.

The teacher walked over and advised us that this was a first for her, and she would give us our grade the next day along with everyone else. I could hardly sleep that night because I had mixed feelings about the production. On one side of the coin, everyone loved the film that saw it; but on the other side, I never got permission to make the movie. I finally fell asleep sometime that night, and it seemed like minutes later, the alarm went off to let me know the morning had arrived, and today was the day my crew and I would discover if our film made the grade! The day went by without a hitch, and everyone was in class awaiting their grades as the teacher began alphabetically. I couldn't wait for her to get to the *H*s because the names of everyone in the crew were further down the alphabet, and they would all hear their grade when she called on me.

It seemed like forever, but then finally, it was my turn! The teacher started out saying in so many words, how this film was very well organized, well filmed, and how the sound track was quality. She then went on to advise the class that I never asked permission to make this film and how the entire class was advised to write a story of our choice consisting of five hundred words or more, and nothing was ever mentioned about producing a film. As my heart sank listening to the teacher's negative comments, I started to drift off thinking how I let my crew down and how we were all going to receive a bad grade on our report card. Suddenly, out of nowhere, like a huge speaker system turned on, I was listening to words bellowing loudly for the very first time. All I heard were these three words coming from the teacher's mouth, "*Never the less*," and she went on to advise the class that the crew and I worked very hard, and she could tell that the production must have taken many hours to complete. Because of this, she will be awarding myself and the entire crew an A+ but advised in the future we should always ask for permission before thinking out of the box.

Needless to say, the crew and I were all very excited, proud, and relieved that this day was almost over, and we were all proud of our A+. We decided to celebrate by using our lunch money to purchase potato chips and sodas at a downtown diner after school. We were all so happy and relieved and wanted to brag about our production to anyone who would listen. I never forgot the excitement that year of stepping outside the box and making my idea become a reality!

40

Dumpsters Aren't All Bad

My dad owned many real estate rentals including residential and commercial. I was in my early teens when the building next door to our corporate office was rented to Frito-Lay, Inc. I think of this story often when I see the Frito-Lay commercials on TV or even when purchasing Frito-Lay products at the grocery store. I remember that day very well because it was my first job, and after the Frito-Lay lease was signed, my dad put me in charge of getting the building ready so the company could move in. I only had two weeks to complete the job, so I started right away carrying out all the trash from the previous renter and throwing it into a big blue dumpster located near the loading dock. I also had to sweep the floors, clean the windows, change all the burned out lights, and give the whole place a fresh coat of paint.

The two weeks went quickly, and I noticed some of the big Frito-Lay semi rigs starting to show up and park near the loading dock. I didn't know if they were waiting on me, or they just arrived early. The next day was D-day, and I had just finished putting on the final touches and started to clean up, when my dad showed up with some big shot, wearing a suit and tie and smoking one of those big fat cigars. I remember this guy well because of the cigar and the scent of old spice aftershave lotion. My dad always wore old spice, which was okay, but when you mix it with cigar smoke, it really stinks. Both my dad and the cigar guy walked around and checked out my work. They looked at the lights and the windows and noticed the floor was especially clean. As they were walking back toward me, I was acting like I couldn't hear what they were saying, but both of them said I did a really good job. Then out of the blue, the guy with the cigar handed me a twenty-dollar bill and said, "Good work, son!"

That was the first tip I ever received. I asked my dad right there if I could keep it and he said absolutely! As I finished cleaning up, I heard the cigar guy say his crew would be back the next day to start unloading the semi rigs. That night, I think I fell asleep going down to my pillow, and the night went by fast because I was so tired from painting. After breakfast the next morning, my mom dropped me off at the office, and I started working on my normal chores, which consisted of sweeping up and emptying trash and organizing the truck garage. Later that day, I noticed the big blue dumpster had been emptied and the guys in their Frito-Lay uniforms were throwing in different size boxes. I was curious and wondered over that way, and while I was peaking in the dumpster, one of the Frito-Lay guys started talking to me, and I asked him what was in the boxes because they were still sealed. He picked up a box and showed me the date on the corner and explained once that calendar date is past due, they have to throw the boxes away. He also told me that a lot of the product is still good for a least a couple of days, but they can't sell outdated product to the public.

    That night, I had a dream about that guy throwing away those boxes and wondered what could be in them. The next day was Saturday, and my brother and I always washed the company trucks and cars on that day. Back then, I earned twenty five cents an hour, and I wanted to work as much as I could because I always felt I was rich on payday. While we were finishing up on the last wash, I ran over to the dumpster and climbed inside to see what mystery was in those boxes. I opened the first box because it was as light as air. It turned out to be a whole box of barbecue potato chips. Since it was near lunch and I was hungry, I tore a bag open, and they were delicious. I advanced to a bigger box, and as I lifted this one, I noticed it was heavy. As I pealed back the cardboard lid, to my surprise, it was filled with gallon glass jars with metal lids. As I pulled one out of the box, I smiled from ear to ear. The gallon size glass jars were filled to the top with beef jerky and each beef jerky was independently wrapped. I love beef jerky, but it is so expensive. Our family would only get it once in a while. I tore into the jar as fast as I could and started eating beef jerky like it was going out of style. I think I may have been in the dumpster close to a half hour eating all the beef jerky and flavored chips I could cram in my stomach. That year, I smuggled beef jerky and chips back to my bedroom and ate a lot of lunches out of the dumpster. I never did tell my dad or my brother about the big blue dumpster. Frito-Lay rented that building for years, and I always loved to work close to the dumpster!

41

Accidental Runover

As I grew older, I advanced from an engine on my bicycle to a real Cushman scooter. I didn't have a driver's license yet, but my dad said if I was careful, I could ride this two-wheeled three-speed rusty-colored scooter, up and down the street. It looked like a big fat bike with a headlight and turn signals. I could only ride it on our dead-end street, but I was still cool! Nobody had a motor scooter like this one. You can imagine how I felt driving by with the wind flying through my hair while kids and grown-ups were watching. As time went on, I got tired of the same old thing, up and down the street. You don't see anything new riding this route all day.

After a few months, I received permission to sell my motor scooter to our paperboy who was of legal age and had a driver's license. The paperboy told me when he was delivering papers on his route, he would always see me riding up and down the street and advised me the scoter would help him a lot on his paper route. I agreed, and we negotiated a price of sixty dollars! The next day, right on time, he delivered the cash all in singles! Sixty dollars back then was huge, and I felt like I was a millionaire. I was rich. I thought I never had to mow a lawn or wash windows or clean out the garage again! Months went by, and I got the itch to have another gasoline vehicle. My brother and I talked my dad into purchasing another Cushman only this time, it was a three-wheeled scooter. You may have seen the model I'm talking about in your own hometown. The police use this type for marking car tires parked by meters on the street. My brother and I had saved up our money and pooled it together to give to my dad. I think the reason my dad had agreed to get the scooter was because my brother had just got his license, and the scooter insurance was cheaper than car insurance.

After the purchase of our new toy, I can't tell you how much fun we both had, and it was faster than anything we had ever driven! This three-wheeled scoter was dressed out with black vinyl doors that would pull shut and snap close in case of inclement weather. The scooter also had a headlight, turn signals, plastic windshield, and a wiper. The back of the scooter resembled a pickup truck with an actual tailgate that opened and shut. My brother would drive the scooter up and down the street while I hid in different trees, waiting for the drive-by, and then launch a cracker ball or two with my sling shot. Cracker balls exploded and were really cool because if I aimed precisely at the plastic windshield, the impact would leave a large black mark after exploding. If I missed the scooter and hit my brother, it would definitely sting, and I would get yelled at. In time, my brother got tired of the scooter and moved into his first car. I inherited the three-wheeled monster. I decided to paint it red, put a piece of carpet in the back end for comfortable rides, and stenciled on both sides, "The Little Red Wagon." This baby was decked out—top speed, full blast down a hill on a windy day, was about thirty five miles per hour! This was a jet compared to the other stuff I drove. I was pretty proud to be the new owner, and in no time, I also received my driver's license. After showing my parents I was a safe driver, and a lot of nagging, they approved driving the scooter straight to school and straight home and don't give any rides. I was in another world!

 I finally got to drive this machine off our dead-end street and onto real city black top. I drove to school a few months and decided it was time for a few of my buddies to sit on the tailgate to see if I could pop a wheelie. We seated about three on the tailgate, and I revved the engine up, popped the clutch, and brought the front end of the Cushman off the ground. The wheelie was a success, but the thing about a wheelie is, once the front end is off the ground, you have no steering, and I almost hit a parked car. I got scared and never tried that again. One windy fall day, I was driving home from school; and as I turned down my street, I noticed my cousin raking leaves in his front yard. My cousin's dad for some reason always kept two stacks of bricks stacked up on one side of his garage. There must have been forty bricks there, and he never did anything with them plus they didn't match any brick on his house. When I was younger playing around outside, I came around the corner and saw those bricks for the first time and went over to check them out. No one was around, so I started to play with them when all of a sudden, the first row started to fall; and I couldn't stop it and then the second row started to fall, and I got scared and ran home.

 Two days later, I came over to play with my cousin, and there they were all stacked up again, nice and neat. From that point on, I figured my uncle must have thought they fell on their own; and every so often when no one was looking, I would tip them over and then run home. Anyway, my cousin must have been out raking for a while because he had a huge pile of leaves probably two feet tall. As I cruised closer, I could see his lips moving, trying to tell me something and pointing at the pile of leaves.

As I got closer, I thought he was saying, "Drive through it. Drive through it!"

No problem, I thought, *this scooter will drive through anything*. A pile of leaves was a piece of cake! I downshifted into second gear to pick up some speed, and as the engine roared, I shifted into third and headed straight for the leaves. I bounced off the road and onto the freshly raked lawn, traveled passed all the shrubs and prepared to hit this huge pile of leaves and watch them scatter in all directions. I couldn't wait because this was such a cool idea! As I hit the huge pile, instead of watching the leaves blow out around me, I felt a thump, and the engine stalled. Little did I know, while my cousin was raking the leaves, he was actually yelling, "My brother's in here. My brother's in here!"

As I looked outside the door and saw my cousin lying under the Cushman scooter, I realized another six inches to the left, and I would have run over his head and probably killed him. I remember him yelling, "Get this thing off of me." As those words bellowed out of his mouth in slow motion, I had already jumped out of the Cushman and was starting to lift it up on two wheels. As I lifted it high with all my might, my cousin crawled out, and I let the scooter crash back down on three wheels. I quickly asked, "Are you all right?" And he remarked he's okay but wanted to go in the house and take a bath. This accidental "runover" scared me to death. I drove the Cushman home, parked it in the garage, and didn't drive it again for over three weeks. The morning after the accident, I awoke with unbelievable pains in both arms. At first, I didn't know what was wrong until I remembered lifting the Cushman up on two wheels. I didn't realize then what adrenalin was, or what it did.

Three weeks later, I did try to lift the Cushman up on two wheels and couldn't budge it. At family reunions, we laugh about what happened back in those days, and my cousin has told his children the story, and so now I'm known as the uncle who ran over their dad.

42

Angels from Heaven

As a young man, I was employed in one of my dad's companies, which owned and maintained house rentals and commercial buildings. In the early years of my grandfather's life, he started purchasing real estate in our hometown and neighboring cities. It didn't matter to him if he purchased commercial buildings, vacant property, or residential homes. He enjoyed building his real estate portfolio.

When my grandfather went home to be with the Lord, my dad and his two brothers inherited the business. I went to work as the low man on the seniority list, but I did have some construction background. I went to work at the office, which was very large and across the street from the river. I remember throwing a pair of my baggy school pants in the river when I went to the warehouse, because my mom said I couldn't have the pegged pants that were in style at the time. I thought if I got rid of the baggy pants, one pair at a time, sooner or later I'd be able to get a pair of pegged pants. Anyway, I was on call, twenty-four seven. Any time something broke, leaked, or needed some type of repair, you could count on me to be there. Not too many people wanted those hours or that job, but I liked to work, and even more, I liked to make money.

My brother and I started very young working for my dad washing beer trucks on Saturdays, and we each received twenty-five cents per hour. Long hours and different types of work were no surprise to me. I remember one summer day in particular; it was so hot you could see the heat waves rising slowly off the blacktop roads, metal roofs, and tops of cars. It was my job that particular day to repair a brick chimney on an older two-story home. After loading up the company truck with tools and equipment I needed, I drove across town to the location and started to unload. As I set the extension ladder up, I immediately noticed the brick chimney was in bad shape. Pieces of mortar were missing, and some of the red brick had actually broken away. I extended the ladder two stories into the sky, just past the roofline, and loaded the first eighty-five-pound bag of mortar mix on my shoulder. As I began to climb the ladder, it seemed the more steps I took, the heavier the bag got. I kept on climbing and finally reached the top of the roof and quickly laid the mortar bag on the hot shingles. I descended back down the ladder several more times to bring up the rest of my tools and supplies.

On the last trip, by accident, I looked down and noticed both ladder hooks never locked the ladder extensions in place. A cold sweat suddenly poured over my face, and I thought to myself, *There is no way I should still be standing on this ladder!* The two sections of ladder were standing up by themselves! If not locked together, the ladder should have slammed down to the ground with me on it, especially carrying an eighty-five-pound bag of mortar. I carefully and slowly climbed back down the ladder holding my breath, taking one step at a time, and hoping it would hold me up on this final decent. It seemed to take forever to get back down to earth. Everything seemed to move in slow motion, and I perspired a small river flowing directly into my eyes leaving a burning sensation. I finally made it to the last rung of the ladder and slowly stepped back to look at the house and imagined what could have happened. I could have been killed! I wiped the sweat off my face and began to lock the ladder into position and finished the day constructing a beautiful resurfaced chimney. At that time in my life, I just blew off the ladder incident and never thought much of it again. I was too young at the time to understand that the good Lord had sent angels to hold the ladder up for me! He needed me on this earth a little longer because he had so much more in store for me.

43

School Fight

My education consisted of private schools. I remember when I started high school. I wore a pair of slip-on penny loafers; but instead of putting pennies in my shoes, I put the shoes in the sink and soaked the tops and stretched the hole out and put in quarters. At the time, our cafeteria lunches were a quarter, so I thought if I ever lost my lunch money, I always had backup in my shoes. I went to gym class for the very first time during my freshman year, and when I came back to shower and change back into my uniform, someone had cut the quarters out of my shoes and left them with pieces of leather hanging down the sides. My mom and dad were furious with me and said it was my own fault and made me wear those shoes for the rest of the year. No freshman looked forward to the dreaded initiation either, and everyone knew you had to go through it because it was the "silent law." If you happened to walk by a restroom on any floor, you could get pulled in by a senior, and then it was all over.

One day, I was walking down the hall minding my own business and got pulled in. Now the seniors had me! After tormenting me, two seniors grabbed my legs and arms, picked me up, dunked my head in a urinal, and screamed, "Welcome to high school." It wouldn't have been that bad if they had just flushed the urinal first. As the rest of the day went on, in an odd way, I felt good my initiation was over. As weeks went by, I became friends with some of the same seniors who initiated me because they found out I had a key to the elevator. My brother's friend, who already graduated, played sports and was injured and couldn't walk the steps, so he was issued a temporary key for the elevator. He never turned it back in after graduation and ended up giving it to me.

During lunch hour, the seniors who smoked would meet me in the basement, and I would unlock the elevator and run it between floors then shut it down while the seniors enjoyed their cigarettes. When they were finished, I ran the elevator up and down the shaft three or four times to air out everything, and we would meet again the next day. I became their best friend who not only ran the elevator but also supplied gum to get rid of the smell and taste of the cigarettes. In exchange, I had protection from anything! I was only a freshman but had an open invitation to their meeting place in the third floor restroom, which consisted of football heroes, wrestler jocks, and me—the gum and elevator provider. One day, we were all up in the third floor restroom with the windows open and noticed a kid from another school talking to one of the senior girls from our school. The athletes started yelling names at the kid when I decided to wad up some toilet paper, get it soaking wet in the sink, and throw it at his car, which was parked below the third floor window. I cleared everyone away from the window, took aim, and launched the wet contraption out the window, through the air, and it splattered dead center on his windshield. It was one of the greatest looking explosions of water and paper I've ever seen!

The senior athletes were bent over laughing so hard they could barely catch their breath. The kid from the other school was standing about six feet away when the toilet paper bomb exploded, and he went berserk. It wasn't like I broke anything on his car; it was just full of millions of pieces of wet toilet paper. The kid looked up and saw everyone laughing with their heads still hanging out of the window and walked like a tough guy to the school entrance. About ten minutes later, the restroom door swung open and hit the wall, and in walked the tough guy. I never thought this guy would actually come inside our school, but here he was and very mean-looking. I stepped back a few feet to stand closer to one of the football players to see what was going to happen. The kid yelled out, "Okay, which one of you jerks threw that mess at my car?"

I almost filled my pants when he yelled and was just about to step forward to apologize when one of the wrestlers stepped forward and said, "I did it. What are you going to do about it?"

Just then, it all broke loose as the kid took a swing at the wrestler, but the wrestler ducked and then picked the kid up and slammed him against the wall. The kid fell down, and all the seniors were laughing and pushing him to the floor as they left the restroom. As they laughed and walked down the hallway, nobody knew his girl friend was writing down all the names of the Seniors who came out of that third floor restroom.

The girl knew I was only a freshman, so she never wrote my name down. The next day was Friday, and while we were in class we heard over the loud speakers of the school that the principal wanted to see the following people in his office immediately. He went on and on, listing the names of the seniors from the list the girl had turned in, and I was sweating it out to see if my name was included. Luckily, my name was never mentioned. Over the weekend, I never thought twice about what happened; but on

Monday, we all got word that those seniors were sent to jail for two weeks. The court house and jail was a block from our school, and the seniors were allowed to go to school but then back to jail at the end of the day. The two weeks seemed to fly by, and none of the seniors ever confronted me for throwing the wet toilet paper bomb out the window. The kid slammed against the wall was hospitalized overnight and then released. A few weeks later, his girlfriend broke up with him, and the elevator and gum business went back in the swing of things for the rest of the year.

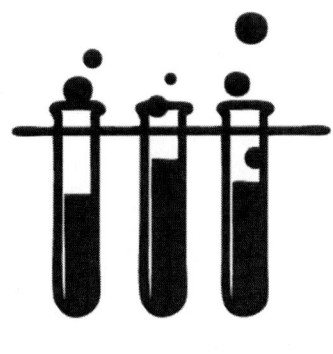

44

Chemistry Class

I remember chemistry class during my freshman year. I thought it was real boring at first! The private school I attended had a policy that all students wore a blazer, tie, and gray trousers. I carried a book with my blazer that I cut out a square on each page and then took my transistor radio apart and fit it into the book. I ran the ear plug cord up my sleeve and into my ear, and no one knew I was listening to music. The girls also wore the same color of blazer, gray skirts, and white top. As a freshman looking at all those skirts gave me an idea. We sat on stools in chemistry class, and I thought it would be cool to take a plastic aspirin bottle, crumble up Alka-Seltzer, and add a bit of water, which would make a compact "water bomb." I had tested the "water bomb" at home several times, so I knew it worked. I took all the necessary parts to school, and when I arrived in class I added the water, shook the bottle a few times, put the top on, and rolled the water bomb under the girl's stools. As the Alka-Seltzer dissolved, it expanded the plastic bottle and blew the cap off spraying a mist all over the girl's legs.

At this point, not knowing what they were feeling, the girls jumped to the floor screaming and pulling up their skirts to their waist to see what was going on. The boys all got a great show for about two minutes and then it was back to looking innocent in a boring class!

45

Unlimited Embarrassment

Private schools have advantages as well as disadvantages. My sophomore year was a disaster! It was tradition at my school that all students wear uniforms consisting of a dark blue blazer, white shirt, tie, gray slacks, and black shoes. The custom-made blazer had to be ordered, which included our school logo, and only two stores in town were authorized outlets. My freshman year jacket fit well because it was a hand-me-down from my brother, but in my sophomore year, I grew and the coat was a little small. My mom thought she would somehow beat the system, so she traveled to another town and bought me a blazer at a discount store. She took the logo off the smaller jacket and sewed it on the new one, and proudly said, "Here you go!" Now this is the lady who bought items on sale and didn't really care if they matched or if it was the wrong color or style, as long as it was on sale, you should be thrilled!

I took one look at the new jacket and boldly yelled, "*No way!*" First of all, it was the wrong color. The jacket was about five shades lighter, and it looked like a girl's jacket. Then after that shock, your eyes automatically noticed it was an "in-your-face double-breasted jacket" with big brass buttons anyone could see a mile away with a logo sewed on a slant. I guess if I was ever lost at sea and a rescue plane flew over, they would notice all the brass buttons reflecting in the bright sun and think I was a floating alien but after further examination would say, "No, it's not an alien. It's some guy wearing a girl's jacket with shiny brass buttons and a crooked logo." This is the same mom who made me dress up like a girl when I was in grade school, to go to a huge scavenger hunt and go door-to-door looking like an idiot. My mom blew her top and explained in a high volume lecture how she had driven all that way to the next town to save money on a new jacket just for me, and I was going to wear it and promptly reminded me that nobody would ever notice. On my first day back to school, I reeked with fear and embarrassment all day long. I can't tell you how many kids in that school stopped and stared as if I was some kind of a freak, and all you heard was laughter in the hallway. The same treatment lasted about two weeks, and I was known as the kid with the jacket. I defiantly don't know how I made it through my sophomore year, but somehow the school year ended, and I still had my sense of humor, and properly disposed of the outlandish jacket in a dumpster where nobody would ever find it. I told my mom I lost it at school, and I would purchase my own jacket next year!

46

Deer Tracks

My grandmother owned a membership in a Michigan camp ground developed for RVs, tents, and cabins. My brother and I were very young the first time we visited the camp ground, but it was an unbelievable experience to say the least! The drive in the car seemed to take forever, and when my brother woke my cousin and me up, I was amazed to see all the trees and sand dunes. The cottages looked like little log cabins, and each camp ground area had about six or seven cabins and then farther down the road was another camp ground with six or seven cabins and so forth. My brother and I swung open the station wagon doors and grabbed our suitcases so we could be the first ones in the door. The walls were made of real logs, and on either side of the stone fireplace were bedrooms with two beds and a dresser, and another two bedrooms at the other end of the cabin. The bathroom included a metal shower, and the vanity was made from logs as well as the kitchen cabinets. The metal shower was built into a solid wall, but there was a small opening at the top all the way to the floor, and that's where I threw my cousin's toothbrush for getting me in trouble while we were on vacation.

It was getting dark, so my brother and I would have to start our exploring in the morning; but in the meantime, my uncle started a fire and piled on the wood while my aunt and cousin went to town to get some groceries. My brother and I set up our bedroom and put our clothes away, made our beds, and washed up for supper. It was cold the first night until the fireplace warmed up the cabin, and then I slept like a log.

The next morning, I was awakened by the fresh scent of bacon and toast. I raced to the kitchen to find my brother already enjoying fried eggs and orange juice. I had this same breakfast at home a thousand times, but when my grandmother prepared it, it tasted even better, and I think it had to do with bacon grease she used in everything, even in our popcorn. After breakfast, my brother and I raced outside, and we were told not to go too far and be back for lunch. I was wearing my green Boy Scout backpack, which included a small canister of plaster of paris I brought from home, an old plastic bowl, some cardboard, a bottle of water, and a bag of peanuts in case I got hungry before lunch. My brother walked over to another camp ground site where he had met a girl by the name of Sheila and was all gaga over her, so I hiked toward the sand dunes; and before long, I was deep into a pine tree forest and following man-made trails. As I came to a car crossing, I spotted deer tracks crossing a dirt road and quickly shook off my backpack and reached inside for my cardboard.

After a few minutes of manipulation, I had transformed the cardboard cereal box into a rectangle form and placed it around the deer track. Using the old plastic bowl, I poured in the last of my plaster of paris followed by just enough water and stirred the contents up with an old twig. As the white creamy substance began to take on a change in texture, I quickly proceeded to pour the contents into my cardboard form. I was so excited to bring back an actual deer track from Michigan to show all the other Boy Scouts in my town. As I waited for the form to dry, I looked around and spotted an old tree with low branches and decided to see how high I could climb. As I ascended up the tree, the view got better and better. When I reached as far as I could climb, I took a minute to take in the view, and I could see forever. I saw fields of pine trees and lakes, sand dunes and smoke from a distant camp fire and the sound of birds chirping in their nest. Off in the distance, I spotted a bright yellow ranger truck making his rounds to the different camp grounds, probably checking to make sure everybody and everything was all right. I was very comfortable, nestled between branches, and continued to watch the ranger proceed down the old dirt road headed my way. I thought it would be cool if he drove right by and never spotted me up in my tree, camouflaged by the green pine tree limbs and huge pine cones. The ranger truck turned the corner and headed right toward my area, and suddenly I remembered, my deer track form, and started down the tree as fast as I could to veer the ranger's truck away from my wet plaster of paris form. I was grabbing every tree limb I could, and my hands were soaking up pine sap as I traveled from one limb to the next. It was a race against time as the ranger truck approached closer and closer.

As I neared the end of my climb, I could finally see the ground and jumped the last three or four feet and ran to the deer track casting area. As I arrived, I could plainly see from a distance that the ranger truck had beaten me to the site, and the cherished deer track was smashed as flat as a pancake, and the ranger not knowing what he had down, continued on to the next campsite. I was very upset as I packed up my gear and started the hike back to the cabin eating a handful of peanuts.

That night, I explained to everyone what had happened; and they advised that later in the week, we could travel in town and get more plaster of paris and try it again. The next day, my brother and I were playing near the cabin and we got into an argument and he pushed me, and on the way down, I hit a tree stump and broke a scab off my elbow, and I began to cry and ran into the woods, holding my arm as the blood dripped on my hand. I don't remember how far I ran into the woods, but I was crying all the way and stumbled upon a large tree that had blown down during a storm. As I sat on the corner of the giant oak cradling my elbow and still crying, I thought it was time to check my injury. As I slowly removed my bloody hand, I noticed the cut wasn't as bad as tearing off the scab. I slowed my crying down to a whimper and as I looked up, within three feet of my face was a full grown deer looking straight into my eyes. The sudden appearance of the deer scared me, and I stopped crying immediately. The deer looked into my eyes for what seemed to be five minutes and then softly walked away minding her own business. I didn't know it then, but as I grew older, I figured the deer must have been a female and heard my crying and sensed I was in pain and walked over to see if she could help.

I never forgot that incident; but when I got back to the cabin that day, no one would believe my story. It was raining the following day, and all the grown-ups were going in town to pick something up and would be right back, but my brother and I got to stay at the cabin. We were told not to go outside and to play with our games. As soon as everyone left, my brother fell asleep on the couch by the roaring fireplace, and I was getting bored. I thought it would be okay to take a walk down to the water, so I opened the back door and made sure there was no noise closing it to wake up my brother. As I ran to the boat docks, I noticed the water was smooth, and I could hear ducks but couldn't see any on the water. I quickly got into a boat and floated out just a few feet from the dock, thinking I could see the ducks better, and I was still safe and close to land. As I sat by myself in the old rusted boat, I could hear the echoing sounds of the ducks and could smell the odor of dead fish in the boat.

As I floated farther away from the dock, I began to look around inside the boat and discovered a fishing pole someone had forgotten and a nice shiny box with all kinds of fishing gear inside. I noticed the fishing pole had an old brown dried up worm still stuck on the hook, so I thought I would try my fishing skills. I tossed the line into the water as I have seen a thousand times on TV. I had never tried fishing before, and I wanted to see what would happen next. I waited for about fifteen minutes, and as I was floating farther away from the dock, all of a sudden, I got a jerk on the fishing pole, and it began to bend as I stood up with excitement. Almost losing my balance in the deep waters with the boat rocking back and forth, I began to reel in this monster, not knowing what I caught. As the splashes got bigger and bigger, I knew the fish was close; and within seconds, I pulled the pole up and brought my catch aboard. As I stood watching my catch flip and flop on the bottom of the boat, I started to wonder how I was supposed to get the fish off the hook. I wasn't about to touch it, so I put my foot on it and pulled as hard as I could, only to tear the fish in half. Scared I was in trouble, I quickly opened the shiny box and grabbed a knife and cut the fishing line and threw the rest of the evidence into the water. Now no one would ever know I had the boat out and caught a fish. As I put the knife back into the shiny case and started to row back to the dock, I noticed I had floated away farther than I thought.

The shoreline was tiny, and I could barley see the camp ground; but twenty minutes or so later, I was getting close. Thinking I was in the clear and having fun fishing, I suddenly heard a car horn, and as I looked, I saw all the grown-ups out of the car and waiting for me to get back to the dock. I stood up to wave, but my uncle told me to sit down and get that boat back to shore. Minutes later, I arrived and got a spanking I'll never forget. I got yelled at for leaving the cabin, for going out in the water, for not having a life vest on, and for using someone else's boat. I was grounded the next day and had to stay in the cabin, and no one talked to me until supper.

The next day, we packed to travel back home, and most of the journey I was worried what my mom and dad would say when they heard the fishing story. But to my surprise, when my brother and I were dropped off at our house, everyone was tired, and not a word was said. I don't know if my mom and dad ever found out, but I still remember the spanking.

47

Uncle Bob

My uncle Bob was a great family man and was always on the leading edge. I remember he had the first Jumping Jiminy's franchise in our hometown, which consisted of black trampoline material, stretched over steel framing in a rectangle hole in the ground, with white concrete curbs surrounding the entire unit. We went there as kids and paid our seventy-five cents for fifteen minutes, and jumped up and down and screamed our heads off until our voices were hoarse. From there, my uncle ventured into one of the first drive-through carryouts he built on the property right next to the trampolines, which became a huge success in our town. When my mom was in a hurry, she would always drive our car into the drive-through and advise my uncle what she needed. He would arrive minutes later with everything in bags.

She paid him, and off we went without ever leaving the car. That was excitement back in those days.

Later on, he purchased a building and opened a huge store in a neighboring town. My mom would get the key on special occasions, like just before school starting, and the whole family would drive over on Sunday after church. The store was closed on Sundays and was about an hour or so from our house.

On the drive over, we always passed a little dinner that had great sandwiches and milk shakes. All us kids knew where it was, and as soon as we saw the tip of the sign through the front windshield as we drove into town, we all said together, "Boy are we hungry!" My mom and dad would start laughing, and my dad would pull the station wagon over and run in to get our food. From the dinner to the store, we always had enough time to eat our food and finish our milk shakes while my mom started her sermon about behaving and not touching anything when we arrived at the store. I heard that sermon a hundred times, and all I was thinking about is how fast can I get to the toy department. My uncle's store was like a Toys "R" Us mixed in with JCPenneys and a little Sears thrown in for hardware items. The store had everything you could think of except groceries.

As the front door was unlocked and the lights turned on, all of us kids took off running though the store, and it was pretty cool to be the only ones there. I always headed straight for the toy section first, because to me, it had the most aisles of hanging toys and large shelves for the bigger items. I know my mom always said don't touch anything, but I was very careful as I opened the package, got the cap gun out, shot most of the enclosed caps that came with the gun, and then sealed it back up. If the toy came with a battery, I would turn it on to see what it would do. Sometimes the toys didn't have a battery enclosed in the package, so I would take the toy over to the battery aisle to see what size it took and played with it and then put the battery back. At the cash register, there were always magazines and candy bars, and sometimes I would get hungry from searching the store and grab a Hershey's candy bar, run to the back room where nobody could see me, and carefully slide out the foil from the wrapper, unwrap one corner so I could break off a couple of squares and then put everything back together again and put it back where I got it. It was like a Christmas wonderland whenever we visited my uncle's store. I had to use the bathroom, which was in the stockroom, and when I was leaving, I had an idea. I thought my brother would be using the bathroom also, so I opened the door just enough for me to squeeze in and stacked a bunch of empty boxes on top of the door so when my brother opened it wide to go inside, the boxes would tumble down on his head. My mom and dad were busy gathering what clothes all of us would need for the new school year, including school supplies and anything they might need, and when finished, they would load it up in the back of the station wagon.

After we got home, my mom and dad would sit down at the kitchen table and write out everything they brought home and next to the item, add the price and then a total for everything followed by a check to my uncle Bob. I guess I got into too many packages on our last visit because my mom received a call from my uncle Bob the next business day, and he was very upset and wanted to know what happened to his inventory. After my mom hung up, she called all of us kids in the kitchen, and I could tell by her voice it could be another sermon. She explained why my uncle was upset and questioned each one of us as if we were seated in a courtroom under oath. As she started her questioning with my sisters and then my brother, I was last and joined in with the denial, which my mom believed. But later that day, I remembered my brother never used the bathroom, so I think all those boxes I had booby trapped for him fell on my uncle Bob's head! I don't know this for sure, but I may have wrecked our visitation rights to my uncle Bob's store because after that phone call, I don't ever remember traveling over there again.

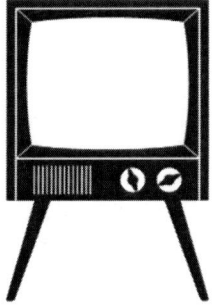

48

The Johnny Carson Show

When it came to our birthdays, my mom would always ask us what we wanted to eat for supper. My response for the first few years, was tacos, because I loved tacos and still do to this day. My mom would agree and then ask how many I wanted, and I would respond millions. A few years later, I acquired a taste for sweet corn and liked the white ears the best; so when it came time for my birthday again, and my mom asked, I would say, *"white sweet corn and no side dishes of any kind, please."*

On my birthday night, I sat down for supper and made sure I had plenty of napkins, while my mom placed three ears of corn on my plate. I grabbed the butter dish and with my yellow corn holders stuck at each end, rolled and rolled the corn in the butter, sprinkled a dash of salt across the top, and dove in, enjoying the start of my birthday meal. I was in heaven, and the fresh sweet corn tasted great; and after eating three ears of corn, my mom would replace them with three more. The one thing I didn't understand at the time was what corn can do to your digestive system. I think if I knew then, I would have slowed down a little; but between the butter, salt, and corn pieces all over my face, I couldn't stop! I ate a total of twelve ears of corn that night, and the next day was a Saturday, which I spent most of it in the bathroom. I thought on my next birthday, I would choose a different meal. The weekend was over, and on Monday, I was back in school with my favorite teacher whom I was in love with. I would stare at her all day long and make believe that I would marry her when I grow up. That dream was crushed one day, when she brought in some guy she called her fiancé, which I had no idea what that meant. After asking my mom that night, I was upset that someone would marry her before I could. The next day, I was still bummed about my teacher but forgot all about it when I noticed a fellow classmate brought in a Necco Wafer house that was built all out of candy. After lunch, I ran back to the classroom and no one had arrived yet, so I walked over to the candy house on display and broke off a Necco Wafer shingle and ate it. I spit the glue out and tried another one, but it tasted the same. Always being curious, I proceeded into the coat room where everyone in the class could hang up their coats and book bags. I wondered what my classmates would be bringing from home and decided to reach in their coat pockets to find out. I checked the pockets to about the halfway point and hit the jackpot. Someone brought three sticks of red licorice to school, and without any hesitation, I promptly jammed all three pieces into my mouth and almost choked but moved swiftly to the next coat. As I traveled all the way to the end of the coats, I didn't find any more treasures. We were getting our report cards at the end of the week, which I always gave to my mom and dad, who would sign it, and then I would take it back the next school day.

Later that week when everyone received their report cards, I looked at the bottom of my card, and there was a U for conduct, which stood for unsatisfactory, and I got scared of how my mom and dad would punish me. I had to think fast because bus eight the banana crate would be arriving soon to take me home. I needed time to think, so I hesitated to leave and fussed with my books as everyone exited the classroom and then my idea sprang into action. Another teacher came up to talk to my teacher at the door, so I raced up to her desk, took her pen she graded the report cards with, and capped the U on my report card, making it an A. Now I felt better and gathered my books and book bag and headed for the bus stop.

When I arrived home and everyone began eating supper, I presented my report card to my mom and dad, and they were very proud of my A. I had a busy weekend playing army with my friends and forgot all about erasing the cap off the A, to change it back to a U. I was surprised my teacher never said anything to me after handing it in, so I figured she never saw the change. The end of the year came quickly, and we were getting our last report card before our summer break. The teacher pulled me to one side and explained I should be ashamed of myself, and I acted like I didn't know what she was talking about. As I sat on bus eight the banana crate on the way home, I opened my report card and almost lost my breath when I saw a note in big red letters across my report card, explaining to my mom and dad just what I had done, and advised I should be reprimanded.

When I arrived home and saw everyone was busy, I went straight to my bedroom and hid the report card; and since it was the last day of school, I was in no hurry to bring up the subject. My mom and dad were getting ready for their newfound love, which was bingo, and advised all of us that my brother was in charge. I think with all the chaos, they forgot about the last report card, and it was at this exact time I felt relieved and wished them luck at their bingo game. They left for bingo after supper and came back late after all of us were in bed.

The next day was Saturday, and I was going through some old boxes in the basement and found an electronic eye kit that I had built years earlier. I used to hook it up on my bedroom door, and the unit would buzz or keep track by numbers; so when returning to my bedroom, I could tell if someone had been there. I realized it was still good for something and thought of an idea that would help me with my mom and dad's bingo game, and they wouldn't know it, but it was going to be a lot of work. I started out in the garage temporarily tying a wire to the top of the automatic garage door opener and carefully hid the wire on the ceiling rafters and then tucked it in running down the wall.

The next phase was getting my dad's hammer and screwdriver and chiseling through the garage foundation, just large enough to slip the wire outside. Thank goodness everyone was gone because the chiseling made quite a noise for about fifteen minutes or so. Once through the garage foundation, I cleaned up the loose pieces of concrete and used the lawn shovel to dig a channel from the garage to the house and quickly buried the wire along with the small concrete pieces eliminating any evidence, and I also made sure I didn't break the sod to show any movement of the grass. I cleaned the shovel off and put it back in the garage. Once the wire was buried to the house, I began the chiseling operation once again to form an access hole into the basement. Breaking through the foundation, I quickly fed the rest of the wire through the hole and into the basement and cleaned up any debris that was left over. I felt better once I was in the basement and could take my time and hide the wire as I traveled from one side of the basement to the other side, stopping directly under my mom and dad's bedroom.

To continue this operation, I would have to wait for another day since it was getting late, and I didn't know who would be arriving back home first, my mom and dad or my brother or sisters. The weekend went by quickly, and I thought about my plan the whole time. Monday was a school day, but I knew on Monday night my mom and dad would be traveling to another bingo game, and I could work in their bedroom without their knowledge or my brother or sisters interfering.

After supper, I got my tools and went into their bedroom and locked the door. I pulled the counsel TV away from the wall so I could get behind it and started back to work with pliers and pulled the carpet back away from the corner. I pounded the screwdriver all the way through the floor for an access hole but had a rough time trying to get it back out. After what seemed to be hours, the screwdriver finally broke loose, and I pulled it out.

From this point, I could see the basement through the hole and quickly put the carpet back and pushed the TV back to the wall. I opened the bedroom door slowly, and with luck, everyone was in the living room watching TV and never heard a thing. The next night after supper, I traveled to the basement and gathered what was left of the wire and pushed it up the hole into my mom and dad's bedroom, and then gathered the electronic eye and components and headed upstairs.

Once in the bedroom, I locked the door again and pulled out the counsel TV and began to wire up one end of the electronic eye kit. Upon completion, I hammered the carpet back down in place and pushed the TV exactly where it was so no one could tell I was ever there. Now that the inside work was completed, I headed out to the garage and wired up the last phase of the project. My plan was to test everything tomorrow night and introduce my brother to the new invention.

The next day, I raced home after school and couldn't wait to finish supper because I knew then that my mom and dad would be leaving for bingo. I had already explained to my brother that I had something exciting to show him, but it would have to wait until they left for bingo. Time seemed to stand still as I watched the clock, and everyone was finishing their supper. My brother and I went into the living room and acted like we were watching TV, and minutes later, my mom and dad left. As soon as the coast was clear, I signaled my brother to follow me to my mom and dad's bedroom. Upon arriving, he asked me what the new invention was, and as I closed the door so no one else could see, I turned on the TV and explained I had wired the electronic eye to their garage door. This meant we could watch TV in their bedroom while they were at bingo, and when they came home and pressed the button in their car to open the garage door, the TV set would shut off. I told him to stay in the room, and I would go to the garage and test the new invention. After I pushed the button to open their garage door, I raced back into the house and found my brother laughing hysterically and said it worked like a charm.

That night, we tested the invention out and closed the drapes to their bedroom, turned on the TV, and went outside to see if we could detect any light coming from the room. With the heavy drapes closed, not one shadow or light beam could be seen, and the first phase of the test was a success. The most important and final test would be if the TV turned off when they got home tonight. My brother and I got ready for bed and then settled into my mom and dad's bedroom, and with the drapes closed as well as the bedroom door, we watched TV and readied ourselves for the final test. We were to be in bed at eight thirty, and it was now eleven thirty; and *The Johnny Carson Show* was on, and so far, everything was fine. We watched and laughed and both of us forgot about my mom and dad coming home until the TV suddenly went off. We both looked at each other and started to laugh and ran to our bedrooms before they could get into the house. The invention was a complete success, and the fun was just getting started. My brother and I watched Johnny Carson every week day for a long time and would brag to other kids at school that we got to stay up to watch the show. They were amazed our parents would let us stay up that late and were jealous they couldn't watch too.

Everything was working like a fine-tuned watch until one night, after the TV shut off and we ran to our bedrooms, my dad walked into the bedroom and accidently dropped his car keys on the carpet. When he bent down to pick up his keys, he put one hand on the top of TV for balance, and the heat alerted him immediately that someone had been in the bedroom. He walked swiftly to my brother's bedroom first, since he was the oldest and in charge. My brother was acting like he was sleeping until my dad turned on the light and began his questioning. Within a few minutes, my brother broke down and spilled his guts to my dad, giving him the whole story of how Harold ran the wire and rigged up the electronic eye and hooked it up to the garage door and the TV. My dad's next stop was my bedroom, and he began the same type of questioning, trying to see if the stories from my brother and I were the same. He drew the conclusion we were both guilty, and my brother and I both got grounded, and both of us had to tear all the wire and components down the next day. Later in life, I would find myself thinking about this story whenever I would watch *The Johnny Carson Show* and wonder what my mom and dad really thought about a small boy dreaming up a plan like this and bringing it to fruition.

I hope you have enjoyed these stories and maybe even cracked a smile or two. Thank you for purchasing volume 1 and keep your eyes open for volume 2 arriving soon!

Synopsis

These are challenging times! Life can be difficult. We struggle with day-to-day situations, setbacks, finances, and rainy days. It's not always easy to be optimistic. No matter where you stand in life, these stories are bound to put a smile on your face! This is your time to sit back, kick your shoes off, and enjoy some good old time stories that may even take you back to memories of *your* childhood! The stories that follow are true! Comical true stories of a child growing up and his mischievous adventures.

About the Author

Harold F. Haaser was born in Fremont, Ohio, a small town between Toledo and Cleveland, and was the second of four children. After serving his term in the United States Marine Corps, he worked in his father's real estate ventures and later went on to work in the resort industry. Harold became a senior vice president and partner in a multimillion-dollar vacation business and resides in Florida with his wife Sheryl. Many times, Sheryl was held in suspense as he narrated one of his many comical stories. As time went on, she suggested those magical times would be worth sharing with others and persuaded him to write a book. After several years of persuading, he did just that.